THE COMPLETE BOOK OF
Chinese Knotting

A Compendium of Techniques and Variations

by **Lydia Chen**

TUTTLE PUBLISHING
Tokyo • Rutland, Vermont • Singapore

Published by Tuttle Publishing, an imprint of Periplus Editions (HK) Ltd, with editorial offices at 354 Innovation Drive, North Clarendon, Vermont 05759, USA, and 130 Joo Seng Road #06-01, Singapore 368357.

Text and illustrations copyright © 1997 Echo Publishing Company Limited and Lydia Chen First Tuttle edition 2007

Library of Congress Control Number 2007920603
10 Digit ISBN: 0 8048 3679 5
13 Digit ISBN: 978 0 8048 3679 1

Distributed by

North America, Latin America and Europe
Tuttle Publishing
364 Innovation Drive
North Clarendon, VT 05759, USA
Tel: 1 (802) 773 8930
Fax: 1 (802) 773 6993
info@tuttlepublishing.com
www.tuttlepublishing.com

Japan
Tuttle Publishing
Yaekari Building, 3rd Floor
5-4-12 Osaki, Shinagawa-ku
Tokyo 141-0032
Tel: (81) 5437 0171
Fax: (81) 5437 0755
tuttle-sales@gol.com

Asia Pacific
Berkeley Books Pte Ltd
130 Joo Seng Road #06-01
Singapore 368357
Tel: (65) 6280 1330
Fax: (65) 6280 6290
inquiries@periplus.com.sg
www.periplus.com

First edition
10 09 08 07 06   10 9 8 7 6 5 4 3 2 1

Printed in Singapore

TUTTLE PUBLISHING® is a registered trademark of Tuttle Publishing, a division of Periplus Editions (HK) Ltd.

Contents

Born first out of practical necessity in ancient times, Chinese knots were soon employed as decorative motifs on artifacts, both functional and ornamental. Between the Warring States Period, when the prototype of the double coin knot evolved, to the Qing Dynasty, to which the plafond knot has been dated, there is ample archaeological evidence that twelve basic knots were developed by Chinese master craftsmen over the centuries before the modern era.

WARRING STATES PERIOD (475–221 BCE)

WESTERN HAN PERIOD (206 BCE–CE 8)

Double coin knot

Horizontal double coin knot on a rubbing taken off a stone carving, Western Han Period, from Feng Lu Jiu's tomb, Tang He, Henan Province.

Prototype vertical double coin knots on a pedestal box from Zhao Qing's tomb, Tai-yuan, Shanxi Province.

Creative Chinese Knotting Designs   115

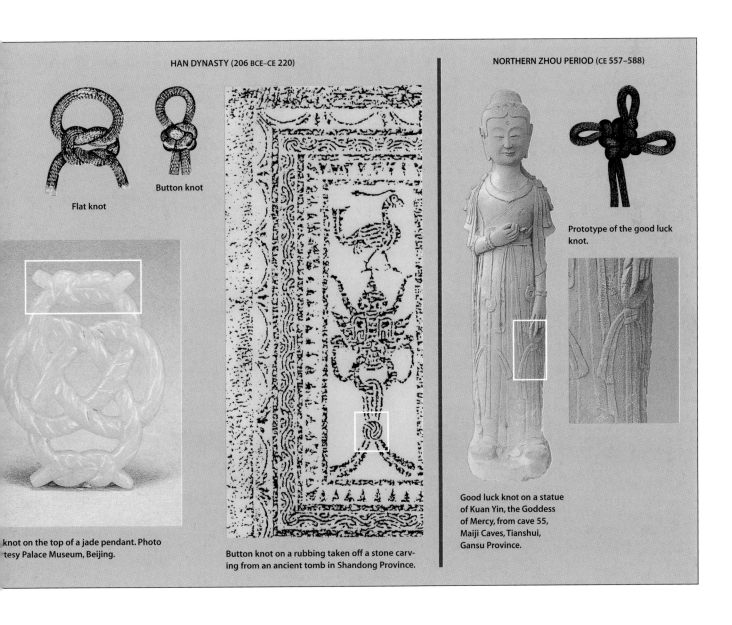

HAN DYNASTY (206 BCE–CE 220)

Flat knot

Button knot

knot on the top of a jade pendant. Photo
tesy Palace Museum, Beijing.

Button knot on a rubbing taken off a stone carving from an ancient tomb in Shandong Province.

NORTHERN ZHOU PERIOD (CE 557–588)

Prototype of the good luck knot.

Good luck knot on a statue of Kuan Yin, the Goddess of Mercy, from cave 55, Maiji Caves, Tianshui, Gansu Province.

A Unique Handicraft

The *Shuowen Jiezi*, the first comprehensive Chinese character dictionary, compiled around CE 100, defines the word "knot" as "the joining of two cords." Knotting is an ancient and highly regarded art form in China and an integral part of Chinese life. Because such knotwork appeared in ancient times, was developed in the Tang and Song dynasties in China and was popularized during the Ming and Qing dynasties, the knots are naturally enough referred to as *Chinese knots*. Moreover, knotting in China spawned a tradition of decorative knotting in other East Asian countries, especially Korea and Japan.

Archaeological studies in China indicate that the art of tying knots dates back to prehistoric times. Recent discoveries include 100,000-year-old bone needles used for sewing and bodkins used for untying knots, proof that knotting existed. Baskets for carrying a multifarious array of goods, ropes for making hunting and fishing snares, lacing for pulling together garments and cords for wrapping and tying items were as crucial to the development of human civilization as spear heads made of flint, boats made of wood and ploughs made of bronze. But, because of the delicate and perishable nature of the materials used to tie knots – mostly fibers from plants and strips of animal hide – few examples of prehistoric Chinese knots exist today. Moreover, the art is generally very poorly documented.

Over the centuries, Chinese knots began to take on a life of their own, eventually being appreciated for their intrinsic beauty in addition to their functional use. Wherever utilitarian knots appeared, decorative knots were not far behind, and nowhere was the art of decorative knotting as highly developed as in Imperial China. A magnificent array of complex

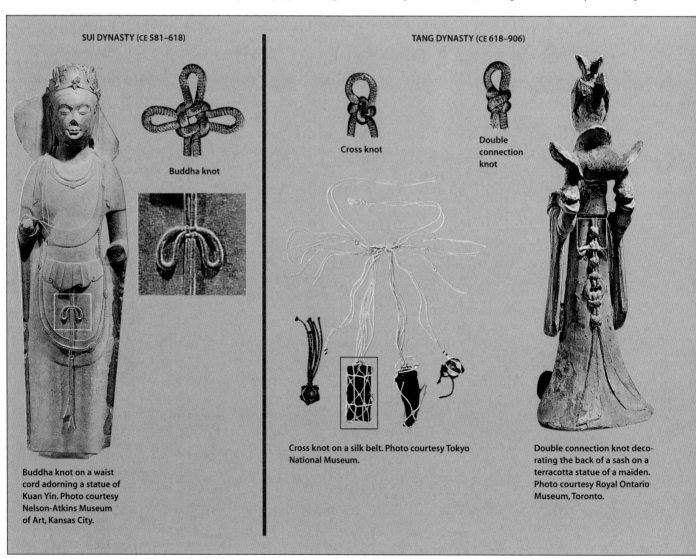

SUI DYNASTY (CE 581–618)

Buddha knot

Buddha knot on a waist cord adorning a statue of Kuan Yin. Photo courtesy Nelson-Atkins Museum of Art, Kansas City.

TANG DYNASTY (CE 618–906)

Cross knot

Double connection knot

Cross knot on a silk belt. Photo courtesy Tokyo National Museum.

Double connection knot decorating the back of a sash on a terracotta statue of a maiden. Photo courtesy Royal Ontario Museum, Toronto.

knots ornamented everything from wind chimes to palace lanterns, sword hilts to teapots, fan tassels to hairpins, and peasant coats to empress's hair. In effect, they were decorations of decorations, imbuing elegance in everything they embellished, including commonplace, everyday items. Some of the best and earliest evidence of these knots has been preserved on bronze vessels of the Warring States Period (475–221 BCE), on silk paintings during the Western Han Period (206 BCE–CE 8) and on Buddhist carvings of the Northern Dynasties Period (CE 316–581). Further references to knotting have also been found in literature, poetry and the private letters of some of the most infamous rulers of China.

The phenomenon of knot tying continued to steadily evolve over the course of thousands of years with the development of more sophisticated techniques and increasingly intricate woven patterns. During the Qing Dynasty (1644–1911), knotting finally broke away from its pure folklore status, becoming an acceptable art form in Chinese society and reaching the pinnacle of its success. Knotting also became an important form of communication, whereby people could express blessings, best wishes, and amorous sentiments. The Chinese pursued knotting ornamentation as a serious art form and devoted enormous amounts of time and effort to perfecting the art. What remains of their work is not only a marvel of technical ingenuity and perfection but a reflection of their creative spirit searching for aesthetic expression.

Knotting continued to flourish up until about 1911 CE, the start of the Republican Era, when China began its modernization process, although some knotting continued into the 1930s, especially in items made for festive occasions and important rites of passage. Due to the effects of industrialization and the Cultural Revolution in China, the art of Chinese knotting, along with many other arts and irreplaceable cultural treasures, was almost lost. However, in the late 1970s, a resurgence of interest occurred in Taiwan, largely due to the efforts of Lydia Chen of the National Palace Museum who founded the Chinese Knotting Promotion Center, as well as the publishers of *Echo* magazine who sought out the few

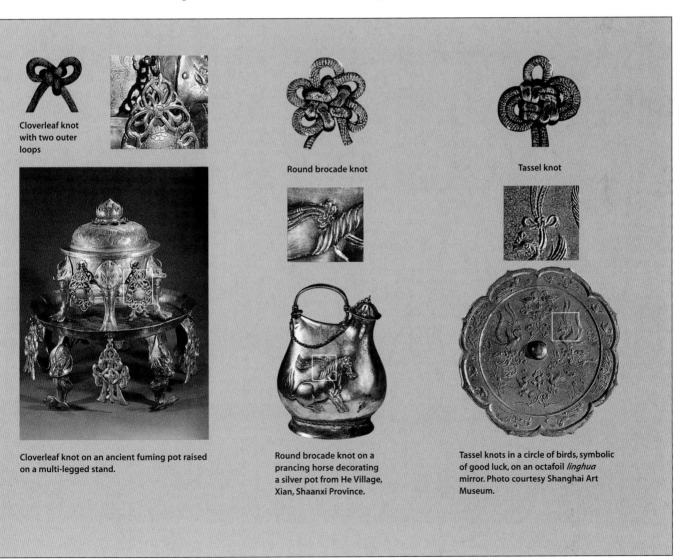

Cloverleaf knot with two outer loops

Round brocade knot

Tassel knot

Cloverleaf knot on an ancient fuming pot raised on a multi-legged stand.

Round brocade knot on a prancing horse decorating a silver pot from He Village, Xian, Shaanxi Province.

Tassel knots in a circle of birds, symbolic of good luck, on an octafoil *linghua* mirror. Photo courtesy Shanghai Art Museum.

remaining keepers of the knotting tradition and recorded their work in a series of articles published in the magazine. When the art of macramé became popular in the West in the 1970s, there was a simultaneous revival of interest in Chinese knots. In the 1980s, Lydia Chen focused her energies on researching the knots embellishing artifacts preserved during the Qing Dynasty, which had been uncovered in archaeological finds, and on historical texts, piecing together scraps of information about the evolution of knots, and then assembling practical manuals to disseminate the art of Chinese knotting to a wider audience. Once an oral tradition, handed down from one generation to another, Chinese knotting became – almost overnight – accessible to millions worldwide, which is testified today by its widespread popularity. Chinese knotting has now become a type of elegant and colorful craft, removed from its original practical use.

In her first book, *Chinese Knotting: Creative Designs That Are Easy and Fun!* (first published by Echo Publishing in 1983 and reissued by Tuttle Publishing two decades later, in 2003), Lydia Chen traces the origins, history and symbolism of Chinese knotting before taking the reader through the fundamental elements necessary for tying Chinese decorative knots – the materials, implements and main processes. Step-by-step instructions are given for eleven basic knots, which provide the building blocks for fourteen compound knots. These are followed by 41 knotting projects of varying difficulty. The book is primarily a compilation of Chinese knots that had almost been lost to time.

In her second book, *Fun with Chinese Knotting: Making Your Own Fashion Accessories and Accents* (first English edition, Tuttle Publishing 2006), the author explores the potential of this traditional art. The book not only entices newcomers to pick up Chinese knotting by focusing on how Chinese knots can be used as fashion accessories (hair ornaments, earrings,

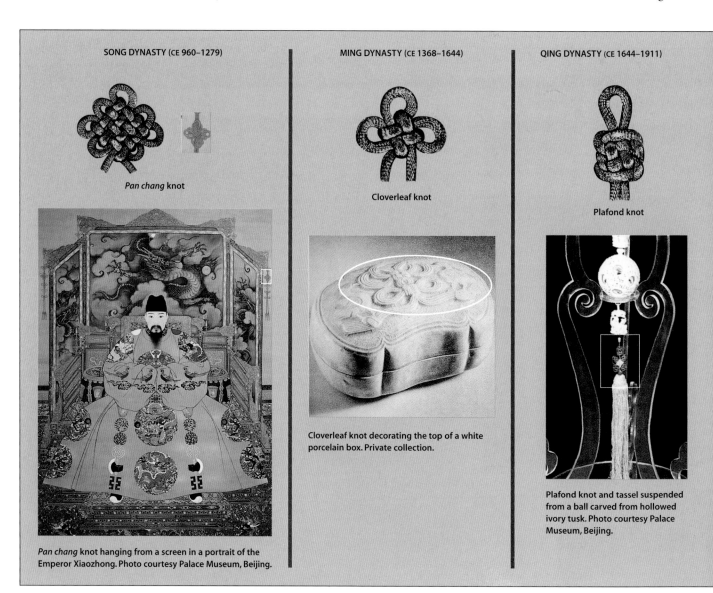

SONG DYNASTY (CE 960–1279)

Pan chang knot

Pan chang knot hanging from a screen in a portrait of the Emperor Xiaozhong. Photo courtesy Palace Museum, Beijing.

MING DYNASTY (CE 1368–1644)

Cloverleaf knot

Cloverleaf knot decorating the top of a white porcelain box. Private collection.

QING DYNASTY (CE 1644–1911)

Plafond knot

Plafond knot and tassel suspended from a ball carved from hollowed ivory tusk. Photo courtesy Palace Museum, Beijing.

necklaces, pendants, brooches, belts, bracelets and rings) and as accents on clothing and other everyday items, but also stimulates them to explore the vast potential of developing new Chinese knots through using innovative cord materials and new color blends, and also by combining Chinese knots. Nine basic knots, nineteen compound knots and five tassel designs form the foundations for making the 135 extraordinary creative applications illustrated in the book.

In this volume, *The Complete Book of Chinese Knotting*, published here for the first time in English, Lydia Chen has condensed almost twenty-five years of untiring research on fourteen basic knots (up from eleven in the first book) into four main methods of tying basic knots. This makes them not only easier to remember but is also more conducive to stimulating creativity. In addition, she has summarized the different ways of modifying basic knots into nine major categories. The variations of the fourteen basic knots may change, but they all fall within the ambit of these nine major modification techniques. Together, they have spurred the creation of another 56 brand-new Chinese knots in this book.

Here also are displayed some of the author's breathtaking original works, which she has created as wall pictures, ornamental hangings and exquisite jewelry to give a different dimension to the art of Chinese knotting. Many of these complex formations are inspired by real and imaginary creatures encountered on early brassware, jade, stone carvings, statuary, paintings, wall murals and mirror holders. Some are created with gold and silver thread – a difficult medium in which to work because of its inelasticity – while others are painted to produce a stiff, sculptural effect. Yet others are designed to project movement and life – a challenge in an art that is essentially symmetrical and static. It is the author's dream to inspire other enthusiasts to broaden the creative horizon of Chinese knotting.

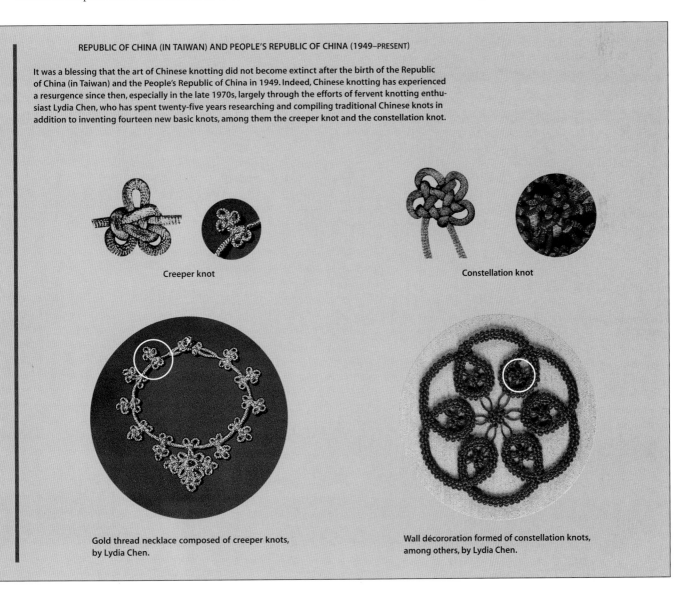

REPUBLIC OF CHINA (IN TAIWAN) AND PEOPLE'S REPUBLIC OF CHINA (1949–PRESENT)

It was a blessing that the art of Chinese knotting did not become extinct after the birth of the Republic of China (in Taiwan) and the People's Republic of China in 1949. Indeed, Chinese knotting has experienced a resurgence since then, especially in the late 1970s, largely through the efforts of fervent knotting enthusiast Lydia Chen, who has spent twenty-five years researching and compiling traditional Chinese knots in addition to inventing fourteen new basic knots, among them the creeper knot and the constellation knot.

Creeper knot

Constellation knot

Gold thread necklace composed of creeper knots, by Lydia Chen.

Wall décoration formed of constellation knots, among others, by Lydia Chen.

Chinese Knots in Ancient Times

Ancient calligraphy from the late Western Zhou Period (770–256 BCE) in the 12th year of Emperor Wei's reign.

Calligraphy from the 27th year of Emperor Wei's reign.

Calligraphy from the 31st year of Emperor Wei's reign.

Jade *xi* tools in the shape of a phoenix and dragon, Warring States Period (475–221 BCE).

Chinese knotting, ancient as it may be, was never the subject of scholarly treatises and there are only passing references to it in the literature. Some scholars believe this is because the early Chinese looked down on science, technology and the folk arts, believing that "Philosophy is the Way, and all others are just tools." Yet, the complexity and ingenuity of the knots that have survived from the late Qing and early Republican periods as well as tantalizing secondhand evidence from sculpture, stone carvings, paintings and poetry testify to the culmination of a long, unbroken artistic tradition that may possibly have predated the written record.

From early times, knotting was one of the most basic skills that Man needed for survival. It was only after knotting techniques were developed to bind two or more things together that he could invent a variety of tools for hunting and fishing, such as bows, arrows and nets. Mankind went on to make farming tools, such as hoes and shovels, by fastening stones to wooden sticks, which led, in turn, to the construction of shelters using cords to bind the different members together, and the development of other inventions to aid production and convenience. Eventually, knotting became developed for communication purposes, to exchange letters and numbers and to record events. The art of knotting gradually found its use in decoration and rituals, firmly establishing itself as an important part of traditional handicrafts.

Using Cords to Record Events

Although it is difficult to envisage, there is sufficient documentary evidence to show that the ancient Chinese recorded events with cords. In a commentary by an early scholar, Zhou Yi, on the trigrams of the *Yi Jing* or *Book of Changes*, the oldest of the Chinese classic texts, which describes an ancient system of cosmology and philosophy that is at the heart of Chinese cultural beliefs, he says that "in prehistoric times, events were recorded by tying knots; in later ages, books were used for this." In the second century CE, the Han scholar Zhen Suen wrote in his book *Yi Zu*, "Big events were recorded with complicated knots, and small events, simple knots." Chapter 81 of the *Tsui Chronicle* also records that "... no writing, hence must carve on woods and tie cords...." Moreover, the chapter on "Tufan" in the *New Tang Chronicle* reveals that due to a lack of writing, the ancient Chinese tied cords to make agreements. This was practiced in other countries as well. For example, in Peru, there was a similar system called "Qui' pu," whereby a single knot means 10, a double knot 20, and multiple knots 100. Special government officials were available to explain the knots. The only indigenous evidence of this practice of making records with knotted cord consists of simple pictorial representations of the symbolic use of knotting on the surface of bronzeware from the Warring States Period (475–221 BCE).

Cords tied in this way show the number of cattle, goats and horses in Okinawa, Japan. This indicates a total animal count of 188.

Knots in Stone Carvings and Fabric Paintings

The double coin knot is the oldest knot to be recorded, although the prototype, a series of vertical double coin knots found on a pedestal box excavated from Zhao Qing's tomb in Taiyuan, Shanxi Province (page 2), appears to be more of a design concept than an actual knot. A stone carving depicting a single dragon and two dragons intertwined at their tails, taken from the relic site of Xianyang Palace, Shaanxi Province, dated to the Qin Dynasty (221–207 BCE), is thought to bear a strong correlation to the fabric painting depicting two dragons in the shape of a double coin knot at Ma Wang's tomb in Changsha, Hunan Province (page 10). More specific correlation can be seen in the recent discovery of stone and brick carvings at the Western Han tombs in Henan Province or the Eastern Han tombs in Shandong Province. In these artifacts, we can see double coin knots in the form of intertwined dragons (page 2) or the intertwined ancient deities Fu Xi and Nu Wo in the form of a human head linked to a dragon's body (page 10). (Nu Wo was the ancient goddess who created Man with mud and cords.) The carving of the intertwined Fu Xi and Nu Wo, besides showing them as the initiator of marriages, also signifies that the Chinese are descendants of dragons. This is one reason why the double coin knot is the love knot popularly referred to in ancient poems. In the stone carvings at an ancient tomb in Shandong, dated to CE 424, Six Dynasties Period, we can see a multiple double coin knot in the form of four intricately intertwined dragons (page 11). Apart from double coin knots, other Chinese knots are depicted in frescoes, for example, the button knot in a stone carving from Shandong (page 3). In terms of structure, the button knot and double coin knot belong to the same system; the former is, in fact, a variation of the latter.

Rubbing from a decorative brick, Han Dynasty (206 BCE–CE 200), from Yang Kuan Temple, Nanyang, Henan Province.

Rubbing from a stone carving depicting the Superior Mother Goddess, Deity Fu Xi and Goddess Nu Wo intertwined in a dragon's body in the shape of a double coin knot, Eastern Han Period (CE 25–220), from Tung Wei Mountain.

Part of a fabric painting depicting two dragons intertwined in the shape of a double coin knot, Western Han Period (206 BCE–CE 8), from Ma Wang's Tomb, Changsha, Hunan Province.

The Poetic Use of Chinese Knots

According to the *Ci Hai* dictionary, a knot is the hook-up of two cords, and hence the knot has always been euphemized as the love between a man and a woman. The famous Tang Dynasty poet Meng Jiao wrote in his poem "Knotting Love":

One knot after another
Knotting true and deep love
Upon my love's departure
I make a thousand knots on his sleeve
I swear to wait faithfully
Hope these knots will prompt him to come home early
But what's the use of tying knots on his garment?
It is better to knot our hearts together
We knot our hearts in whatever we do
We knot our hearts for eternity

The love knot has always been synonymous with true love. The *Ci Hai* goes on to explain that "In ancient times, gold cords were intertwined countless times to signify true love, and thus were appropriately euphemized as the love knot."

Among Chinese knots, the double coin knot most resembles the love knot, another reason for us to extrapolate that the love knot mentioned in ancient poems is actually today's double coin knot. Indeed, the love knot is the earliest knot mentioned in ancient poems, such as "Yu So Si" by Emperor Liangwu of the Southern Dynasty, "So Yi" by one of China's most renowned poets, Li Bai, "Willow" by Liu Yu Xi, "Farewell Song" by Wang Jian, "Spring in Wulin" by Ou Yang Siu and "To the Pipa Girl" by Li Qun Yu. In each case, the poet revealed his love with the love knot. In *Meng Liang*, Wu Zhimu wrote that in ancient marriages, the red cloth covering the bride's face was graced with a double love knot, as were the bride and bridegroom's wine cups, which were quickly drained and turned upside down under the bed for good luck.

Besides the love knot, there is the happy together knot mentioned in Emperor Liangwu's poem "The Autumn Song." We do not know what the happy together knot looks like. However, the *History of the Liao Kingdom* mentions that every year, on May 5th, the Liao people tied cords of five different colors on their arms and called this the happy together knot. Given that the Han and Liao used their knots for different purposes, the two happy together knots may be altogether different.

There is a third knot that is quite similar to the love knot, the pair knot. In his poem "Jie Yang Chang," Jie Xi Si of the Yuan Dynasty mentioned the pair knot. Also, Li Bai, in his poem "Dai Zheng Yuen," talked about another knot which he euphemized as the *huiwen* knot. It is likely that this *huiwen* knot is actually the love knot, a case of a single entity with two names.

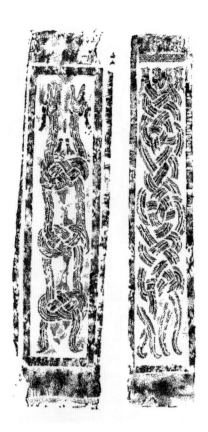

Rubbings of stone carvings from an ancient tomb in Changsan, Shandong Province, showing multiple double coin knots in the shape of intertwined dragons, Six Dynasties Period (CE 265–589).

Detail of a painting, Five Dynasties Period (CE 907–960).

Detail of a painting, "Li Gao Listening to Ruan," Song Dynasty (CE 960–1279).

Knots in Everyday Life

Through China's long history, knotting gradually developed into a distinctive decorative art, generating countless fashion, household and ritual items used in royal temples, palaces and in the homes of common folk, and also to make a special occasion even more wonderful. Knots were cherished not only as symbols, but also as an essential part of everyday life, and were used to decorate lanterns, musical instruments, fans, dresses, chopsticks, sachets and many other items.

Prior to the Han Dynasty (206 BCE–CE 220), Chinese knots, though limited to the double coin knot and its derivative, the button knot, commonly graced the jade and copper ornaments (page 12) as well as mirrors (page 14) and seals. Long strings of jade secured with knots on an Eastern Zhou Period (770–256 BCE) wooden figure from the Chu tomb, Xinyang, Henan Province (page 14) testify to an even earlier decorative knot-making tradition in China.

The decorative function of Chinese knots became more pronounced in the Six Dynasties Period (CE 265–589), as seen in the pillar depicting three consecutive double coin knots and a compound double coin knot comprising four interlocking dragons in the Southern Dynasty tomb in Changsan, Shandong (page 11).

Chinese knotting peaked during the Sui and Tang dynasties (581–906), when numerous basic knots – sauvastika, cross, round brocade and tassel – and one that looks like a cloverleaf with two outer loops – were used to adorn palace objects. In the ensuing Song Dynasty (960–1279), these single knots were replaced by multiple knots. The true cloverleaf knot also appeared. Though none of the present day knots appeared in the late Song–early Yuan dynasties, this period had one very unique decorative knot, the *pan chang*, an early example being the strand of *pan chang* knots on the screens behind imperial portraits (page 6). We do not see a lot knots adorning everyday objects in the Ming Dynasty (1368–1644).

The Qing Dynasty (1644–1911) witnessed a second peak in the use of knots. During this time, all present day basic knots became widely used. We can even see some outer loops being extended into complicated knots.

Buddhist statue, Western Wei Dynasty (CE 535–556), from cave 102, Maiji Caves, Tianshui, Gansu Province.

Copper ornament, Han Dynasty 206 BCE–CE 220).

Right: Stone carving entitled "The Empress's Devotee," Northern Wei Dynasty (CE 386–534), in Bingyang Cave, Longmen Grottoes, Luoyang, Henan Province.

Far right: Portrait entitled "Seated Folks," Southern Song Dynasty (CE 1127–1279). Photo courtesy Palace Museum, Beijing.

Clothing

Long robes with flowing sleeves, the traditional garb of both men and women in ancient China, had to be fastened at the waist with knotted sashes. Simple examples exist in paintings (pages 11 and 12). Gentlemen of the Zhou Dynasty (c. 1050–256 BCE) would carry a special device, a *xi* (page 9), tied to their waist sashes for untying knots. They were also fond of wearing elaborate belt ornaments hung from their sashes, composed of several small pieces of delicately carved jade with cord eyelets strung together with intricate knotwork.

Tang sculpture has preserved the designs of a handful of knots, some quite complex, that have survived to the present day. The prototype of the good luck knot (with only one layer of overlapped outer loops) can be seen in a hanging tassel on a statue of the Goddess of Mercy, Kuan Yin, dated to the Northern Zhou Period (page 3). Subsequently, the Buddha knot, designed after the ancient Indian motif which Buddhists hold as a symbol of all good fortune, was spotted hanging from the waist of another statue of Kuan Yin, dated from the Sui Dynasty, now in the Nelson-Atkins Museum of Art, Kansas City (page 4). The double connection knot was first discovered decorating the back of a sash on a Tang terracotta figure housed in the Royal Ontario Museum, Toronto (page 4). On the same tassel is a Buddha knot. Indeed, a few double connection knots with outer loops, of which the knotting technique still remains elusive, are apparent on various stone Bhodisattvas from the Western Wei and Northern Qi periods (mid-sixth century). An elegant knot was found on the tassel of the empress's devotee on the stone carving of the same name found in Bingyang Cave, Luoyang (page 12). The cross knot made its debut on a Tang Dynasty silk belt in the Tokyo National Museum. The image on page 4 shows a net bag tied from cross knots.

In the Southern Song portrait "Seated Folks" (page 12), some double connection knots with outer loops are clearly visible on the characters, but the knotting technique still eludes us. Since it only appears around the Southern Song–early Yuan period, it can serve as a diagnostic indicator for other artifacts.

Detail of a portrait, "The Lady with the Fan," Tang Dynasty (CE 618–906).

Rubbing of the "Seven Scholars of the Bamboo Garden," rubbing from a brick frieze, Danyang, Jiangsu Province.

Stone frieze entitled "The Emperor Praying to Buddha," Bingyang Cave, Longmen Grottoes, Luoyang, Henan Province.

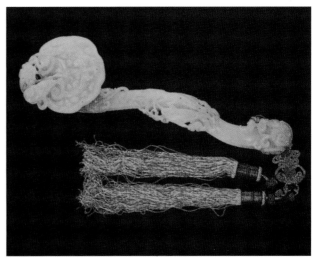

Ru yi (sacred fungus) knot, Tang Dynasty (CE 618–906). Photo courtesy Palace Museum, Beijing.

Furniture and Other Household Objects

Bronze mirrors, forged with rings on the back, were tied to walls by knotted cords (page 14), while bronze vessels from the Warring States Period, replicas of earthenware jugs, were decorated with a knotted network resembling the cords used to support their fragile antecedents. In various portraits from the Tang and Five Dynasties periods, Chinese knots occur beneath chairs, for example, in "The Lady with the Fan" (page 13), and in screens behind emperors' seats. In fact, the first *pan chang* knot was found in a portrait of the Ming Emperor Xiaozhong (page 6). From the Song period, Chinese knots were used to decorate armrests. The predilection for Chinese knots is evident in all portraits of Song royalty, for example, Empress Zheng Zhong (page 14).

Accessories and Other Items

Umbrellas adorned with Chinese knots are abundant in the "Luo Goddess" scrolls dated from the Eastern Jin Period. They are also seen in the stone frieze, "The Emperor Praying to Buddha," in the Bingyang Cave, Luoyang, Henan (page 13). Musical instruments embellished with knots can be seen in the brick frieze, "The Seven Scholars of the Bamboo Garden," from Hu Bridge in Danyang, Jiangsu (page 13). During the Qing Dynasty, knots were widely used to grace objects in daily use such as *ru yi*, sachets, wallets, fan tassels, spectacle cases and rosaries. All existing basic knots, except the creeper and the constellation knots, also appeared on ornaments from the Qing Dynasty, regarded as the heyday of Chinese knots, where the outer loops were extended into other knots. As a decorative design on objects, the round brocade knot was first discovered on a Tang silver pot dug up in He Village, Xian (page 5). The tassel knot was discovered on a Tang mirror (page 5) and the cloverleaf knot on a Song porcelain box (page 6).

Portrait of the Empress Zheng Zhong, Song Dynasty (CE 960–1279).

Longevity mirror, Han Dynasty 206 BCE–CE 220). Photo Courtesy of Palace Museum, Beijing.

Painted wooden figure, Eastern Zhou Period (770–256 BCE), from the Chu tomb, Xinyang, Henan Province.

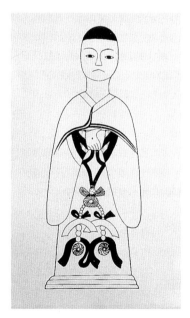

Sketch of the same wooden figure.

Special Characteristics
of Chinese Knots

In the realm of knotting, Chinese knots are considered to have the most outstanding decorative value. Even the Japanese and Koreans – themselves masters at tying knots – are fascinated by the knotting techniques and applications of the Chinese for the simple reason that the structure of Chinese knots is highly varied and their applications limitless.

Chinese knots are not only exceptionally graceful but are also practical: they can tie objects tightly. A major characteristic of Chinese knotwork is that all the knots can be tied using one cord, usually about a meter in length. Another is that every basic knot is named according to its distinctive shape, meaning or pronunciation. A Chinese knot body is made up of two layers of cords sandwiching an empty space, hence the three-dimensional, symmetrical body is tough enough to stay in shape when suspended. Redundant cord ends can be hidden inside a knot body and ornamental beads, precious stones or other embellishments can be incorporated for additional aesthetic effect. Since all Chinese knots are identical on both sides, they are pleasing to the eye.

Chinese knots also have unlimited variations due to their complicated weaves and weave sequences, the number of outer loops employed, the tightness of the knot body, etc. Furthermore, the basic knots can be randomly recombined to form many more patterns. All Chinese knots can be used to decorate and tie objects. The scope of ingenuity in Chinese knotting is thus without boundaries.

Knotted gold thread pendant by Lydia Chen.

Chinese knot wall décoration by Lydia Chen.

Knotted masterpiece by Sekishima Noboru.

A study in simplicity and elegance by Sudou Kumiko.

A wall hanging made of flat knots and rolling knots, courtesy of Tanaka Toshiko.

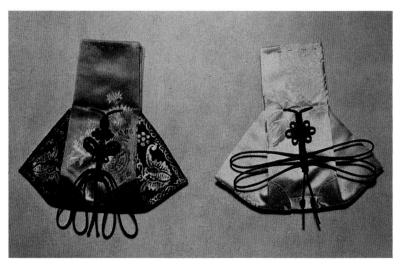

Korean examples by Kim Ju-shen.

A stunning knot encircling a bead by Lydia Chen.

In his book *Japanese Gift Wraps*, Sekishima Noboru expounded that the Japanese tradition of tying knots, *hanamusubi* (*hana* means "flower" and *musubi* "knot") was, in fact, a legacy from China's Tang Dynasty. This occurred in the seventh century when the Japanese Emperor, impressed with the elegance and practicality of the reed and white jute cord knots used to tie a gift from the Chinese, encouraged his people to adopt the same practice. However, the Japanese knots that developed as a result tend to be comparatively austere and formal, perhaps because of the constraints in Japanese tradition and the overall Japanese aesthetic. Up to this day, Japanese knots are still fairly simple and structurally loose and are more decorative than practical in function. They are embedded in everyday activities such as wrapping. The use of numerous colors and diverse types of cord are particular Japanese characteristics.

Closely related to Chinese knotting is *maedup* or Korean knotting. As with Japanese knots, it is believed that Korean knotting techniques originated from China. According to the late Kim Ju-shen, one-time president of the Korean Handicraft Association, historical data about Korean knots is grossly lacking and their origin and use in ancient times is unclear although it appears that they are based on Chinese antecedents. However, Korean knots have evolved into a rich culture of their own in terms of design and color and the incorporation of local characterstics. The main differences between Chinese and Korean knots are the proportion of tassel to knot (much longer tassels are used in Korean knots), the type of cord used (Koreans favor round braided cord), and color (Koreans tend towards the five primary colors of red, yellow, green, blue and black and often use all five in a single knot).

Unlike Chinese knots, Western knots, the best known ones being the two-dimensional flat knot and curled knot, are very simple and repetitive – almost monotonous. Not a great deal of skill is needed to tie them. Moreover, they are neither particularly decorative nor useful for tying objects. Since there is little skill involved in Western knotting, any outstanding example that is produced must have a unique theme and an intricate blend of colors and materials.

Chinese Knotting Techniques

Fourteen basic Chinese knots are treated in this book, namely the (1) cloverleaf knot, (2) *pan chang knot*, (3) round brocade knot, (4) constellation knot, (5) good luck knot, (6) Buddha knot, (7) double connection knot, (8) plafond knot, (9) flat knot, (10) creeper knot, (11) double coin knot, (12) button knot, (13) cross knot and (14) tassel knot. These basic knots have numerous, almost unlimited permutations, which can be formed either from variations of their basic designs or from a combination of basic knots. The knotting techniques for producing many of these so-called compound knots were taught in *Chinese Knotting: Creative Designs That Are Easy and Fun!* and *Fun with Chinese Knotting: Making Your Own Accessories and Accents*. In this book, four major methods or techniques for tying knots and nine ways of modifying them are applied to each of the fourteen basic knots. Each basic knot is treated separately, with its various modifications derived from the major methods and modification skills clearly shown in words and pictures. Not only will this strategy enable you to learn the knotting techniques of many new knots, but it will also allow you to fully appreciate the concept of basic knots and lead you to create new knots yourself.

Four Main Methods of Tying Basic Knots

From lengthy research into the knots that were first used by the Chinese for practical purposes and later as decorative motifs, Chinese knotting experts, including Lydia Chen, the author of this book and a world-renowned knotter, have identified fourteen basic knots, namely the (1) cloverleaf knot, (2) *pan chang* knot, (3) round brocade knot, (4) constellation knot, (5) good luck knot, (6) Buddha knot, (7) double connection knot, (8) plafond knot, (9) flat knot, (10) creeper knot, (11) double coin knot, (12) button knot, (13) cross knot and (14) tassel knot.

These fourteen basic knots have been classified not only according to their structure but also the four main methods or techniques used to tie them, which include (1) pulling and wrapping outer loops, (2) using single flat knots, (3) overlapping outer loops and (4) knotting semi-outer loops or "S" curves.

1. Pulling and Wrapping Outer Loops

Cloverleaf Knot

This is made by forming first one loop, then a second loop and passing it through the first one, then forming a third loop and passing it through the second one. The cord end is pulled tight to form the center knot. The cord sections between the inner loops make up the outer loops of the knot.

Pan Chang Knot

This knot is formed using the cloverleaf knotting technique, but increasing the number of outer loops on each side to two or more. The cord end is hooked up with the fourth side of outer loops two times or more using the same technique as the cloverleaf knot.

Round Brocade Knot

This involves the cloverleaf knotting technique, but an additional outer loop is pulled through every second or more outer loop in front of it. The second last outer loop is then hooked up with the first two loops in the beginning using the pull one, wrap one technique.

Constellation Knot

This knot is formed using the round brocade knotting technique, except that the second outer loop in the beginning is wrapped around the first. The rest of the outer loops are done in the usual pull one, wrap one technique. The last two outer loops are then hooked up with the first two outer loops, also using the pull one, wrap one method.

Good Luck Knot

This is tied using the cloverleaf knotting technique, but after pulling the cord end through each outer loop, the cord end is reversed and pulled through each outer loop again to make it look as though the knot is being tied with two cords. The difference between a good luck knot tied this way and one done using the overlapping outer loop method is that the cord ends will come out of the knot body in a slightly different position.

 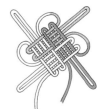

2. Using Single Flat Knots

Buddha Knot

This is made of two flat knots, with the second knot hooking through the loop of the first. The cord between the two knots becomes the top loop.

Double Connection Knot

One cord end is used to tie a single flat knot around the other cord end, then the other cord end is used to tie a single flat knot around the first cord.

Plafond Knot

The body of this knot is made by hooking up and tightening four consecutive single flat knots using both cord ends.

Flat Knot

This is formed of two opposing single flat knots pulled together.

Creeper Knot

This knot is made by tying two opposing single flat knots, then pulling the cord section on the top part into the body of the knot.

3. Overlapping Outer Loops

Double Coin Knot

This knot involves making two loops, one on top of the other, with a third loop weaving through the other two to hold them together.

Button Knot

This involves overlapping the outer loops of two opposing knots. The right outer loop with the cord end beneath it is put on top of the left outer loop. The right cord end is then woven clockwise around the overlapped loops.

4. Using Semi-outer Loops or "S" Curves

Cross Knot

This knot takes the shape of two "S" curves weaving their way into each other to form the body of the knot.

Tassel Knot

This is basically a double cord cross knot with compound outer loops to produce a double-layered structure.

NINE WAYS OF MODIFYING BASIC KNOTS

Modified knots are variations of basic knots. Although the finished knots may appear to be quite different from the basic knots from which they originate, they can nevertheless be traced back to the skills employed in tying the basic knots. In this section, nine major ways or methods of modifying basic knots are described and illustrated, namely (1) increasing the number of outer loops, (2) altering the knotting sequence of the outer loops, (3) extending the outer loops, (4) overlapping the outer loops, (5) changing the shape and reducing the cords, (6) shifting the weave of the knot body, (7) knotting a tall three-dimensional knot, (8) recombining skills and (9) recombining basic knots.

The names of the techniques provide a clue to the way in which each basic knot is modified. Naturally enough, the more complicated the basic knot, the more potential it has for modification. Hence, some basic knots have more modified knots and some fewer.

The examples given below will help you appreciate the basic principles in modifying basic knots as preparation for the next section on extending and varying basic knots.

1. Increasing the Number of Outer Loops

With basic knots that are tied using the "pull and wrap" technique, for example, the cloverleaf knot, round brocade knot, good luck knot, constellation knot and *pan chang* knot, the number of outer loops involved in the pull and wrap can be increased to make knots of different sizes with varying numbers of outer loops.

Round brocade knot with six outer loops.

Round brocade knot with ten outer loops.

Brooch in the form of a round brocade knot with eight outer loops.

2. Changing the Knotting Sequence of the Outer Loops

For all Chinese knots formed by overlapping, pulling and wrapping, for example, the cloverleaf knot, round brocade knot, *pan chang* knot, constellation knot and good luck knot, a change in the sequence of the overlap, pull and wrap is all that is needed to produce modified knots with overlapped outer loops. For example, follow a 1, 3, 2 sequence instead of 1, 2, 3. There are plenty of illustrations on this point in "Creative Chinese Knotting Designs" on pages 115–159.

Round brocade knot with ten overlapped outer loops.

Round brocade knot with ten overlapped outer loops.

Round brocade knot with ten compound outer loops.

Pan chang knot with its compound outer loops shifted.

3. Extending the Outer Loops

With the round brocade knot, cloverleaf knot or constellation knot, where the outer loops are tied using the "pull and wrap" method, the outer loops can be deliberately extended whereby whenever an outer loop meets another, the former is pulled through and wrapped around the latter. The new knots made in this way have more complicated weaves than the original basic knots, and are known as the compound round brocade knot, compound cloverleaf knot and compound constellation knot.

The dotted lines indicate the forward extension of the outer loops.

Cloverleaf knot with four outer loops wrapped and pulled.

Cloverleaf knot with four outer loops. The outer loop is wrapped forward.

Cloverleaf knot with four outer loops. The outer loops are pulled and wrapped forward.

Cloverleaf knot with four outer loops. The outer loop is pulled and wrapped forward.

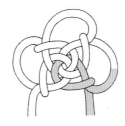

Cloverleaf knot with four outer loops. The outer loop is wrapped, pulled and wrapped forward.

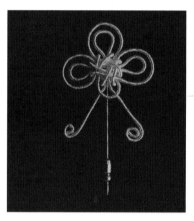

Wall decoration made from a good luck knot in which two outer loops were overlapped after every two interspacing loops.

4. Overlapping the Outer Loops

A good luck knot is made by overlapping the outer loops clockwise or anticlockwise. The more outer loops involved, the bigger the hole in the center of the knot body. To rectify this, two outer loops can be overlapped after every two, three or more interspacing loops. In this way, the hole will shrink and the knot body thicken.

Good luck knot with four outer loops.

Good luck knot with six outer loops. The two outer loops are overlapped after every two interspacing loops.

Brooch made from a good luck knot with four compound loops.

The first layer of outer loops in this good luck knot are overlapped in the usual way. However, for the second layer, the outer loops are overlapped after every one, two or three outer loops to produce compound outer loops, giving the knot the name good luck knot with compound loops.

Good luck knot with four outer loops.

Good luck knot with four compound loops.

Brooches made from good luck knots with overlapped side loops.

The first layer of outer loops in this good luck knot are overlapped in the usual way. Before overlapping the outer loops in the second layer, the side loops around the knot body are lengthened and overlapped to form new basic knots. Slightly different new knots can be devised by varying the direction of the lengthening process, the face from which the side loops are lengthened and the direction of the overlap.

Good luck knot with four outer loops.

Good luck knot with overlapped side loops.

The outer loops in the good luck knot can be arranged longitudinally and latitudinally as in the *pan chang* knot, although they are tied according to the usual good luck knot technique, to produce a new basic knot which has a *pan chang* knot body but, at the same time, outer loops of varying sizes. This new basic knot is called the *pan chang* good luck knot.

Good luck knot.

Pan chang good luck knot.

Hanging decoration made from a *pan chang* good luck knot.

5. Changing the Shape and Reducing the Cords

The knot body of a *pan chang* knot is always formed by pulling and wrapping the outer loops on all four sides, be it a triangular or a polygonal knot. The right cord end always weaves through the outer loops, and the left cord end always wraps the outer loops. The last side involves the "pull and wrap'" process. When a *pan chang* knot is made using only three sides of its outer loops, there will be changes in the shape of the knot body and outer loops. This produces a new type of *pan chang* knot called the *pan chang* knot with reduced cords.

Pan chang knot.

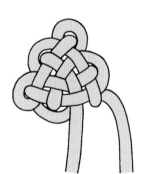

Modified *pan chang* knot (triangular *pan chang* knot).

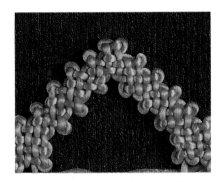

Corner of an ornament made from a modified *pan chang* knot.

Pan chang knot.

Pan chang knot with reduced cords.

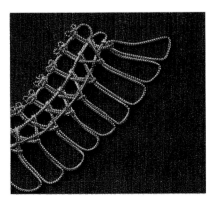

Wing of a phoenix made from a *pan chang* knot with reduced cords.

6. Shifting the Weave of the Knot Body

Normally, the body of a *pan chang* knot comprises a straight latitudinal and longitudinal weave. But if the longitudinal cord is twisted 90 degrees (or 180 degrees) to a latitudinal direction (or, in this case, anticlockwise), with the unfinished weave being replaced by other cords and additional cords put in the center of the fixed weave, then a new type of *pan chang* knot, called the shiftweave *pan chang* knot, is formed.

Hanging decororation made from a 90-degree shiftweave *pan chang* knot.

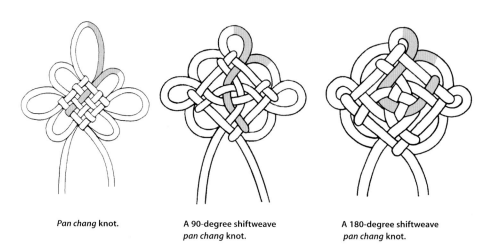

Pan chang knot.

A 90-degree shiftweave *pan chang* knot.

A 180-degree shiftweave *pan chang* knot.

7. Tying a Tall Three-dimensional Knot

Most Chinese knots consist of two "faces" sandwiching an empty space. The three-dimensional effect of this is not particularly pronounced and indeed often goes unnoticed by most knotters. The concept of tying a tall three-dimensional knot was conceived in 1985 when it was discovered that certain parts of some knots can be used much like outer loops.

There are basically three knotting techniques for making tall three-dimensional knots. The first is where the cord ends are hooked up with the completed outer loops or a certain part of the cord in the knot body and knotted as vertically as possible in the knot body.

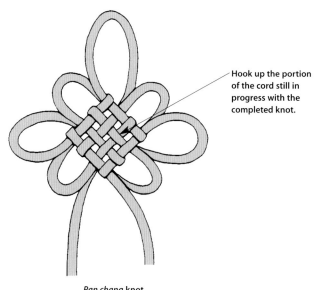

Hook up the portion of the cord still in progress with the completed knot.

In this ornamental hanging, the portion of the cord still in progress has been hooked up with the completed knot to achieve a 3D effect.

Pan chang knot.

The second type is where the exposed cord of the knot body is tied into another knot to produce a stereoscopic effect. Structurally, the button knot and *pan chang* knot are highly suitable for making into tall three-dimensional knots.

Three-dimensional button knot.

Hanging ornament in the form of the Chinese "longevity" character made from a 3D button knot.

The third type is when the starting point of the knot is changed, for example, using the center of the *pan chang* knot body as the starting point.

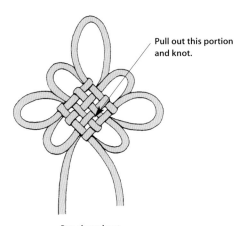

Pull out this portion and knot.

Pan chang knot.

Three-dimensional knot made from this technique.

8. Recombining Skills

Two or more variation skills can be used to tie a new knot. For example, shifting the weave of the knot body combined with altering the knotting sequence of the outer loops can be applied to a shiftweave *pan chang* knot with both overlapped and compound outer loops. Or altering the knotting sequence of the outer loops can be combined with the *pan chang* good luck knotting technique to produce a *pan chang* good luck knot with overlapped and compound outer loops.

A 90-degree shiftweave *pan chang* knot.

Pan chang knot with compound outer loops.

Pan chang knot combining a 90-degree shiftweave and altering the sequence of the outer loops.

Hanging knot in the form of a *pan chang* good luck knot made using recombination techniques.

9. Recombining Basic Knots

There are two ways of recombining basic knots, one being the technique of knotting with both cord ends, a method which first appeared on artifacts from the Han Dynasty (206 BCE–CE 220). The other way, which first appeared on artifacts from the Qing Dynasty (CE 1644–1911), is to knot with a single cord end. The various recombining skills are summarized below.

Chainlink Technique

This simply involves tying a series of single knots of the same kind. After the first knot has been tied, the remaining cord is used to tie a second knot, third knot, and so on. Regardless of whether the knots are being linked vertically, horizontally or in a circle, it is just a matter of linking them to form a larger formation without changing the shape of the individual knots.

Bracelet made from a vertical chainlinked plafond knot.

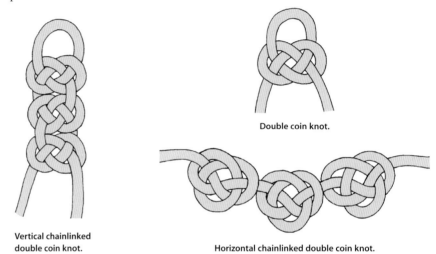

Double coin knot.

Vertical chainlinked double coin knot.

Horizontal chainlinked double coin knot.

The Use of Outer Loops

A Chinese knot is made up of a knot body and its surrounding outer loops. As long as the body of the knot is firm, not loose, outer loops can be formed and utilized in a variety of ways. Indeed, from the beginning of the Qing Dynasty until around 1985, all the modified knots that were developed were based on this principle.

There are four main ways of using outer loops. The first involves the use of a single outer loop. Once the cord end leaves a knot body, it can be tied on an outer loop to form another knot. Beads can also be threaded on the cord end to enhance the knot.

Ru yi earrings made from cloverleaf knots using the method of making use of a single outer loop.

Round brocade knot.

Using a single outer loop of a round brocade knot.

The second involves the use of multiple outer loops. During the knotting process, once the cord end leaves a knot body, it can be pulled, wrapped, overlapped or hooked up with one or more completed outer loops.

Ornamental knot made by hooking up multiple outer loops.

Combination cloverleaf knot and *pan chang* knot.

Hooking up the outer loops of a cloverleaf knot and a *pan chang* knot.

A third technique involves sharing outer loops. Sometimes, when a few knots are linked together, an outer loop may be shared by two or more knots to form a bigger modified knot.

Knot formation made using the technique of sharing outer loops.

Cloverleaf knot with four outer loops.

Sharing outer loops within a cloverleaf knot.

The fourth technique is cutting the outer loops of a knot. As it is a cord end that produces a knot, the more cord ends, the bigger the potential for knotting variations. In this technique, some very long outer loops are tied, then cut in the middle (or any part thereof) to make more cord ends for tying more variations.

Knot formation made using the technique of cutting the outer loops of a round brocade knot.

Round brocade knot.

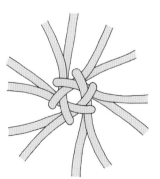

Cut outer loops of a round brocade knot.

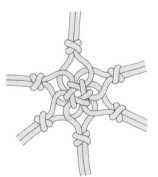

New knots tied to the cut outer loops of a round brocade knot.

EXTENSIONS AND VARIATIONS OF BASIC KNOTS

Quite a few modified knots were taught in the author's *Chinese Knotting: Creative Designs That Are Easy and Fun!* and *Fun with Chinese Knotting: Making Your Own Fashion Accessories and Accents*. This book, after classifying the nine major variation skills, goes on to further analyse each of the enriched variations.

Each basic knot has its own unique characteristics and the number of variations that can be derived from each basic knot also differs. In this book alone, there are 56 new modified knots. Each is accompanied by step-by-step drawings and instructions for making the various knots. Photographs of the finished knots are also provided.

Examples

Ear Loops and Outer Loops

In this book, a portion of a shuttling cord is called an **ear loop**, while a loop around the knot body is an **outer loop**.

There are two types of ear loops. One is the type that shuttles left and right or up and down, such as the ones that make up the cloverleaf knot. The other type is a circle, like the ones used in the double coin knot.

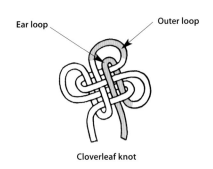

Cloverleaf knot

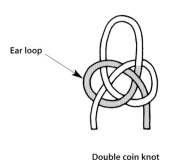

Double coin knot

Good Luck Knot: Front and Back of First Layer

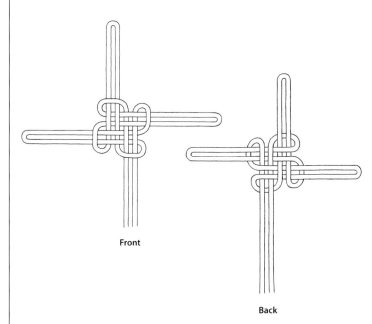

Front

Back

Shiftweave Pan Chang Knot: Pull One, Wrap One, Pull Two, Wrap Two Method

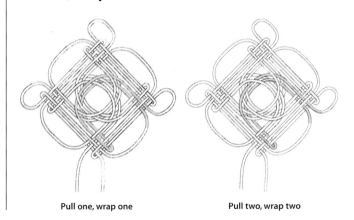

Pull one, wrap one   Pull two, wrap two

Cloverleaf Knot with Three Outer Loops: Ear Loop Pull and Wrap Method

Each ear loop is marked with a number. ① means the first ear loop, ② means the second and so on.

The plus sign (+) indicates wrapping the cord around an outer loop and the minus sign (−), indicates pulling the cord through it.

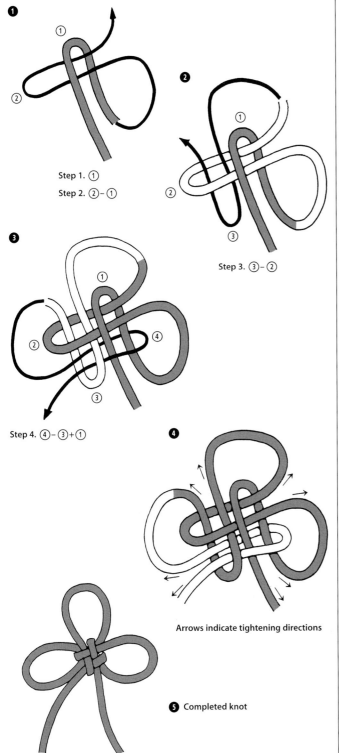

Step 1. ①
Step 2. ②−①

Step 3. ③−②

Step 4. ④−③+①

Arrows indicate tightening directions

❺ Completed knot

Double Coin Knot: Ear Loop Overlap Method

The right ear loop weave is indicated by ① and the left ear loop weave by − ①.

The plus sign (+) means going over the cord section encountered while the negative sign (−) indicates going under the cord section encountered.

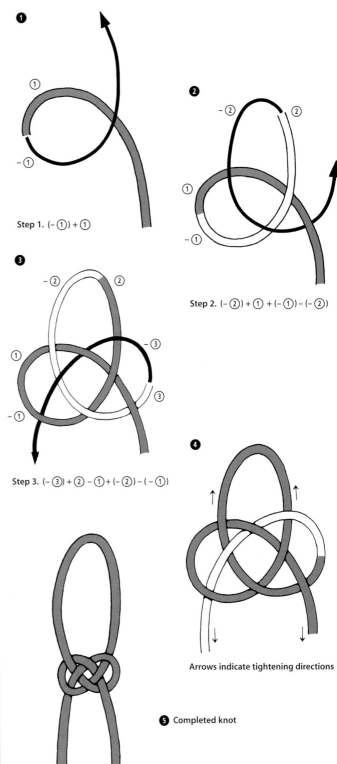

Step 1. (−①) + ①

Step 2. (−②) + ① + (−①) − (−②)

Step 3. (−③) + ② − ① + (−②) − (−①)

Arrows indicate tightening directions

❺ Completed knot

Looping

In the case of the round brocade knot, the greater the number of outer loops, the bigger the central hole. If a smaller central hole is desired along with with a multitude of outer loops, the number of loops looped to the next outer loop must be increased.

Example: Looping every second outer loop in a round brocade knot wth six outer loops.

Example: Looping every third outer loop in a round brocade knot with six outer loops.

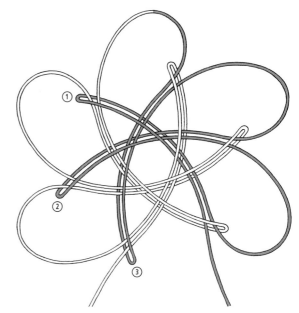

Step 1. ①
Step 2. ② – ①
Step 3. ③ – ① – ②

Step 1. ①
Step 2. ② – ①
Step 3. ③ – ① – ②

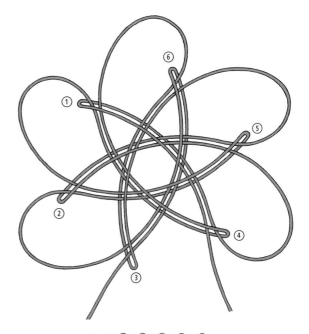

Step 4. ④ – ② – ③
Step 5. ⑤ – ③ – ④ + ①
Step 6. ⑥ – ④ – ⑤ + ① + ②

Step 4. ④ – ① – ② – ③ + ①
Step 5. ⑤ – ② – ③ + ④ + ②
Step 6. ⑥ – ③ – ④ – ⑤ + ③

Cloverleaf Knot

Regardless of the number of outer loops involved, the tying technique of the cloverleaf knot always involves pulling an outer loop through the outer loop immediately in front of it until the last outer loop is reached, when that is pulled through the one immediately in front of it and then hooked up with the first outer loop. Different types of modified cloverleaf knots are shown below.

Modified Knots

Increasing the Number of Outer Loops

In theory, the number of outer loops in the cloverleaf knot can be increased infinitely. However, once the fourth outer loop is made, the central hole becomes too large and makes the knot body too loose. Hence, the multiple outer loops in a cloverleaf knot must be pulled tight and used as a ring.

Changing the Knotting Sequence of Outer Loops

You can tie a cloverleaf knot with overlapped outer loops similar to a round brocade knot with overlapped outer loops simply by changing the knotting sequence of the outer loops. Since this knot is structurally simple, there is not much variation.

Cloverleaf knot with multiple outer loops.

Cloverleaf knot with overlapped outer loops.

Modified Knot Bodies

Modifying the Outer Loops

The knotting technique of a compound cloverleaf knot involves extending the outer loops of the basic knot by pulling and wrapping an outer loop with another one that it encounters. However, since there are two types of structure to the cloverleaf knot, one being pull one, wrap one and the other being wrap one, pull one, and at the same time there can be a change in the knotting sequence in the whole knotting process, it is possible to come up with two types of compound cloverleaf knots, namely Type 1 and Type 2. In order not to confuse readers, only the different types of knots with marked structural differences are introduced here.

Type 1(a) Compound cloverleaf knot (see page 33).

Type 1(b) Compound cloverleaf knot (see page 34).

Type 1(c) Compound cloverleaf knot (see page 35).

Type 1(d) Compound cloverleaf knot (see page 36).

Type 2(a) Compound cloverleaf knot (see page 37).

Type 2(b) Compound cloverleaf knot (see page 38).

Type 2(c) Compound cloverleaf knot (see page 39).

Type 2(d) Compound cloverleaf knot (see page 40).

Sharing Ear Loops

Both the *pan chang* knot made with a reduced number of cords and the constellaton knot are examples of modified knots made from a few cloverleaf knots with two outer loops sharing some ear loops. You can use the ear loop sharing technique to link a few knots, thus making a bigger and more elegant knot. Below are a few types of modified knots made by linking four cloverleaf knots with two outer loops (you can also try three outer loops). Because of the different methods of sharing long ear loops, it is possible to come up with two types of modified cloverleaf knots: wrap one, pull one as well as wrap two, pull two.

Type 1 Cloverleaf knot with opposite corners sharing an ear loop (see page 41).

Type 2 Cloverleaf knot with opposite corners sharing an ear loop (see page 42).

Type 3 Cloverleaf knot with opposite corners sharing an ear loop (see page 43).

Type 1 Cloverleaf knot with adjoining sides sharing an ear loop (see page 44).

Type 2(a) Cloverleaf knot with adjoining sides sharing an ear loop (see page 45).

Type 2(b) Cloverleaf knot with adjoining sides sharing an ear loop (see page 46).

Type 3(a) Cloverleaf knot with adjoining sides sharing an ear loop (see page 47).

Type 3(b) Cloverleaf knot with adjoining sides sharing an ear loop (see page 48).

Type 1(a) Compound Cloverleaf Knot

This is made from the basic cloverleaf knot using the technique of pulling and wrapping the next loop. Extend an ear loop and wrap around the next loop it encounters.

TYING INSTRUCTIONS
Step 1. Make ear loop 1 as shown below. **Step 2.** Pull ear loop 2 through 1. **Step 3.** Pull ear loop 3 through 1 and 2 and wrap around 1. **Step 4.** Pull ear loop 4 through 2 and 3 and wrap around 1 and 2.

HINTS
When tightening the knot, pull the cords firmly so that the central body does not become loose. At the same time, make sure the cords lie flat and do not twist, bend or kink. Gently pull the slack out of the outer loops. If tied properly, the knot will be highly elegant and slightly three-dimensional in appearance.

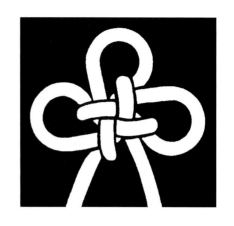

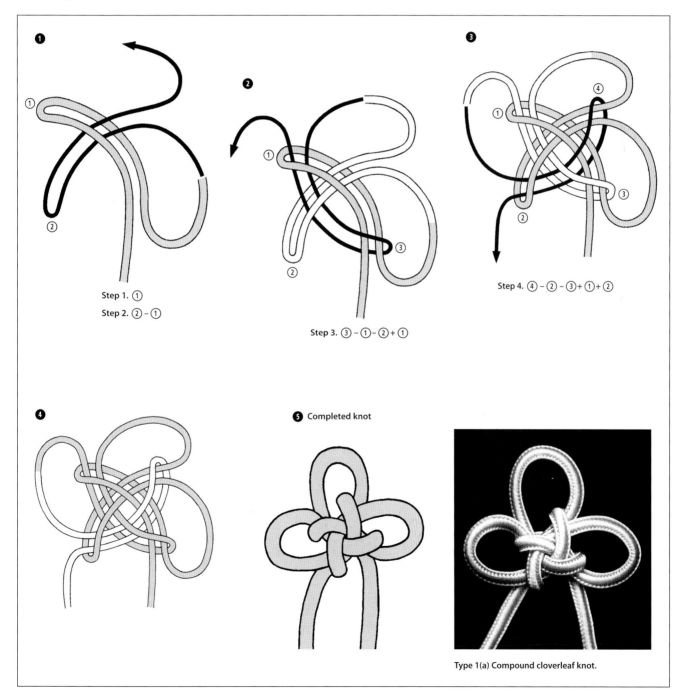

❶

Step 1. ①
Step 2. ② – ①

❷

Step 3. ③ – ① – ② + ①

❸

Step 4. ④ – ② – ③ + ① + ②

❹

❺ Completed knot

Type 1(a) Compound cloverleaf knot.

Type 1(b) Compound Cloverleaf Knot

This is made from the basic cloverleaf knot using the technique of pull one, wrap one. Extend an ear loop, pull through the next loop it encounters, and wrap around the second loop.

TYING INSTRUCTIONS
Tie the knot following the step-by-step illustration guide below.

HINTS
See page 33.

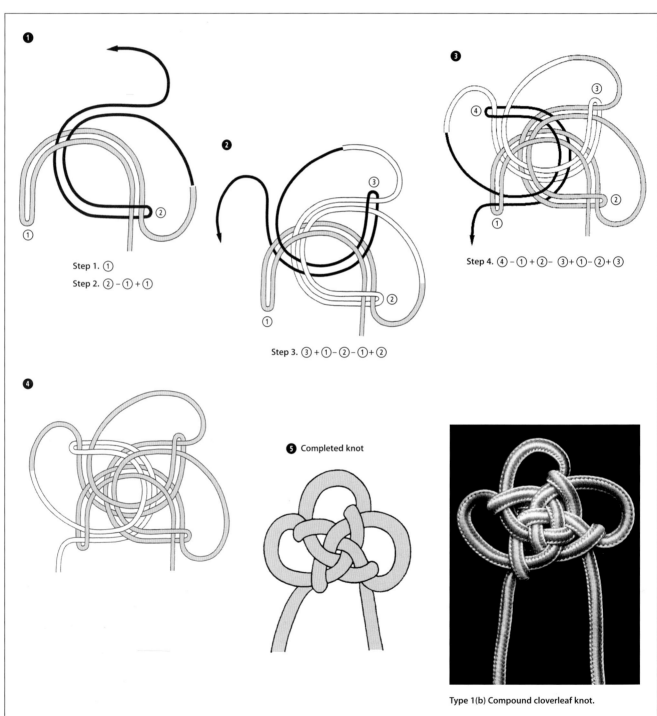

❶

Step 1. ①
Step 2. ② – ① + ①

❷

Step 3. ③ + ① – ② – ① + ②

❸

Step 4. ④ – ① + ② – ③ + ① – ② + ③

❹

❺ Completed knot

Type 1(b) Compound cloverleaf knot.

Type 1(c) Compound Cloverleaf Knot

This is made from a basic cloverleaf knot using the technique of pull one, wrap one. Extend an ear loop, wrap around the next loop it encounters, pull through the second loop and wrap around the third.

TYING INSTRUCTIONS
Tie the knot following the step-by-step illustration guide below.

HINTS
See page 33.

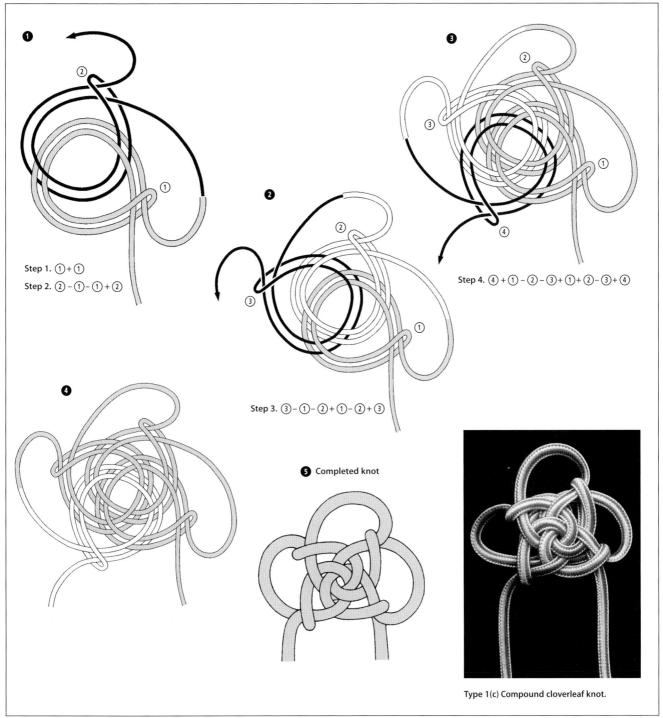

❶

Step 1. ① + ①
Step 2. ② − ① − ① + ②

❷

Step 3. ③ − ① − ② + ① − ② + ③

❸

Step 4. ④ + ① − ② − ③ + ① + ② − ③ + ④

❹

❺ Completed knot

Type 1(c) Compound cloverleaf knot.

Type 1(d) Compound Cloverleaf Knot

This is made from a basic cloverleaf knot using the technique of pull one, wrap one. Extend an ear loop, pull through the first loop it encounters and wrap around the second and third loops.

TYING INSTRUCTIONS
Tie the knot following the step-by-step illustration guide below.

HINTS
See page 33.

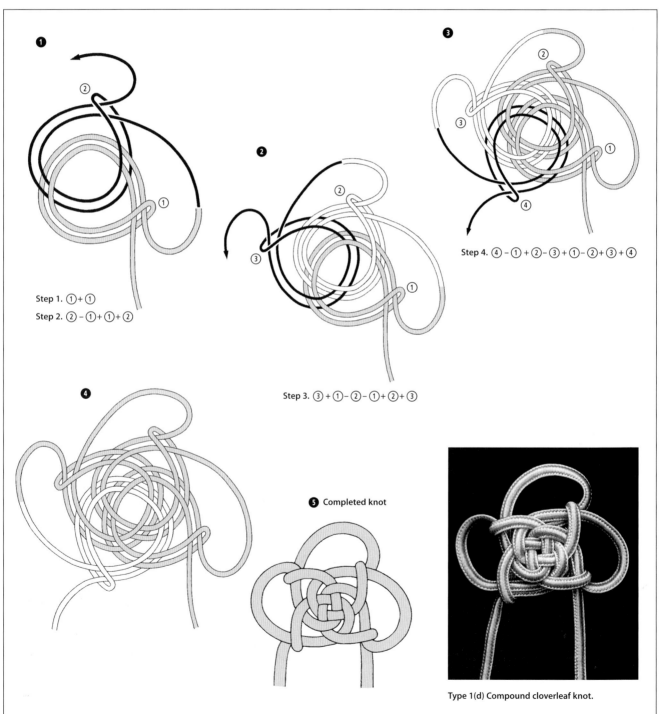

❶

Step 1. ①+①
Step 2. ②−①+①+②

❷

Step 3. ③+①−②−①+②+③

❸

Step 4. ④−①+②−③+①−②+③+④

❹

❺ Completed knot

Type 1(d) Compound cloverleaf knot.

Type 2(a) Compound Cloverleaf Knot

This is made from the basic cloverleaf knot using the technique of wrap one, pull one. Extend an ear loop, then wrap around the first loop it encounters.

TYING INSTRUCTIONS
Tie the knot following the step-by-step illustration guide below.

HINTS
See page 33.

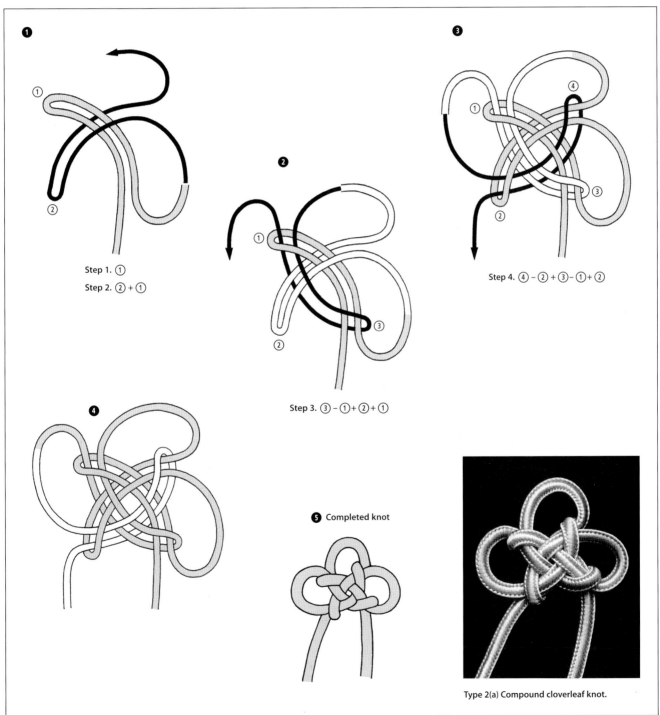

Step 1. ①
Step 2. ② + ①

Step 3. ③ − ① + ② + ①

Step 4. ④ − ② + ③ − ① + ②

⑤ Completed knot

Type 2(a) Compound cloverleaf knot.

Type 2(b) Compound Cloverleaf Knot

This is made from the basic cloverleaf knot using the technique of wrap one, pull one. Extend an ear loop, wrap around the first loop it encounters, pull through the second loop, then wrap around the third.

TYING INSTRUCTIONS
Tie the knot following the step-by-step illustration guide below.

HINTS
See page 33.

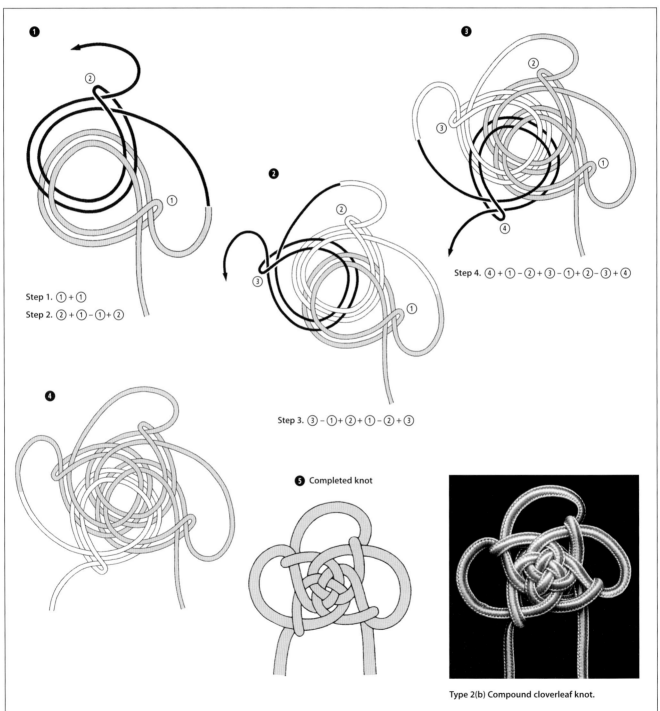

①

Step 1. ① + ①
Step 2. ② + ① − ① + ②

②

Step 3. ③ − ① + ② + ① − ② + ③

③

Step 4. ④ + ① − ② + ③ − ① + ② − ③ + ④

④

⑤ Completed knot

Type 2(b) Compound cloverleaf knot.

Type 2(c) Compound Cloverleaf Knot

This is made from the basic cloverleaf knot using the technique of wrap one, pull one. Extend an ear loop, then wrap around the first and second loops it encounters.

TYING INSTRUCTIONS
Tie the knot following the step-by-step illustration guide below.

HINTS
See page 33.

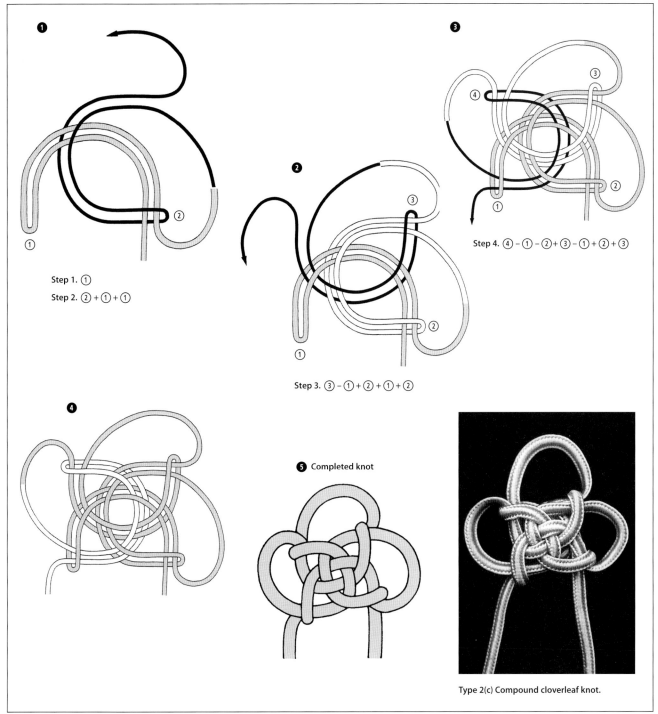

Step 1. ①
Step 2. ② + ① + ①

Step 3. ③ – ① + ② + ① + ②

Step 4. ④ – ① – ② + ③ – ① + ② + ③

❺ Completed knot

Type 2(c) Compound cloverleaf knot.

Type 2(d) Compound Cloverleaf Knot

This is made from the basic cloverleaf knot using the technique of wrap one, pull one. Extend an ear loop, pull through the first loop it encounters and wrap around the second loop.

TYING INSTRUCTIONS
Tie the knot following the step-by-step illustration guide below.

HINTS
See page 33.

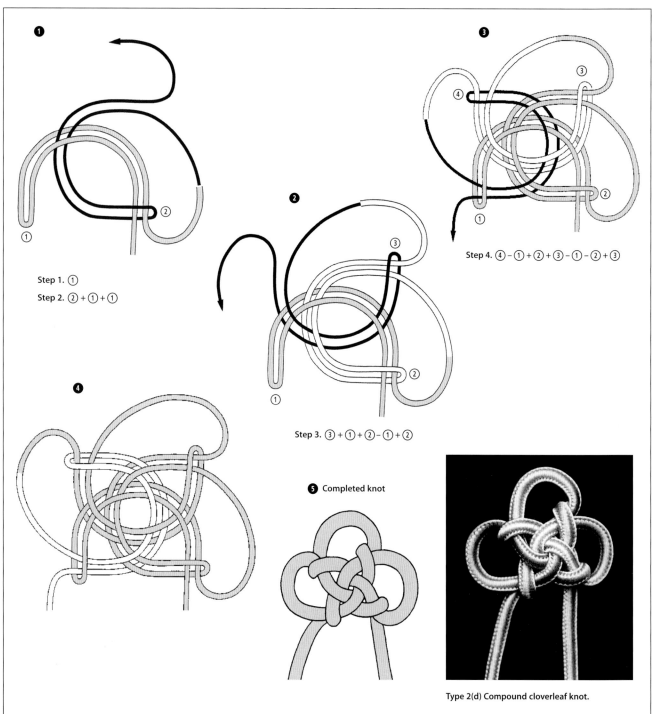

❶

Step 1. ①
Step 2. ② + ① + ①

❷

Step 3. ③ + ① + ② − ① + ②

❸

Step 4. ④ − ① + ② + ③ − ① − ② + ③

❹

❺ Completed knot

Type 2(d) Compound cloverleaf knot.

Type 1 Cloverleaf Knot with Opposite Corners Sharing an Ear Loop

Take the straight line in opposite corners and apply the wrap one, pull one sharing technique.

TYING INSTRUCTIONS

Step 1. Make ear loop 1 as shown below. **Step 2.** Do the same for ear loop 2. **Step 3.** Wrap ear loop 3 around ear loops 2 and 1. **Step 4.** Wrap ear loop 4 around ear loop 1. **Step 5.** Pull ear loop 5 through ear loop 1. **Step 6.** Pull ear loop 6 through ear loops 3, 1 and 2 and wrap around ear loop 3. **Step 7.** Pull ear loop 7 through 6 and wrap around 3. **Step 8.** Pull ear loop 8 through 1, wrap around 4, pull through 6, wrap around 3, pull through 5 and wrap around 1.

HINTS

• First tighten the four cloverleaf knots with two outer loops to prevent the formation becoming loose. As far as possible, arrange the entire formation into a circle.

• The newly combined central knot body is the main focus. You can make different parts tighter or looser according to taste and to produce different effects.

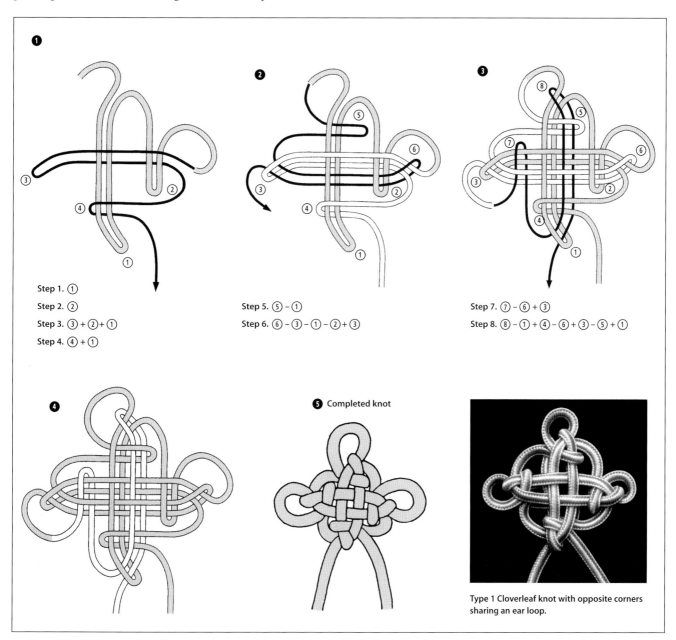

Step 1. ①
Step 2. ②
Step 3. ③ + ② + ①
Step 4. ④ + ①

Step 5. ⑤ − ①
Step 6. ⑥ − ③ − ① − ② + ③

Step 7. ⑦ − ⑥ + ③
Step 8. ⑧ − ① + ④ − ⑥ + ③ − ⑤ + ①

⑤ Completed knot

Type 1 Cloverleaf knot with opposite corners sharing an ear loop.

Type 2 Cloverleaf Knot with Opposite Corners Sharing an Ear Loop

Take the curved line in opposite corners and apply the wrap one, pull one sharing technique.

TYING INSTRUCTIONS
Tie the knot following the step-by-step illustration guide below.

HINTS
See page 41.

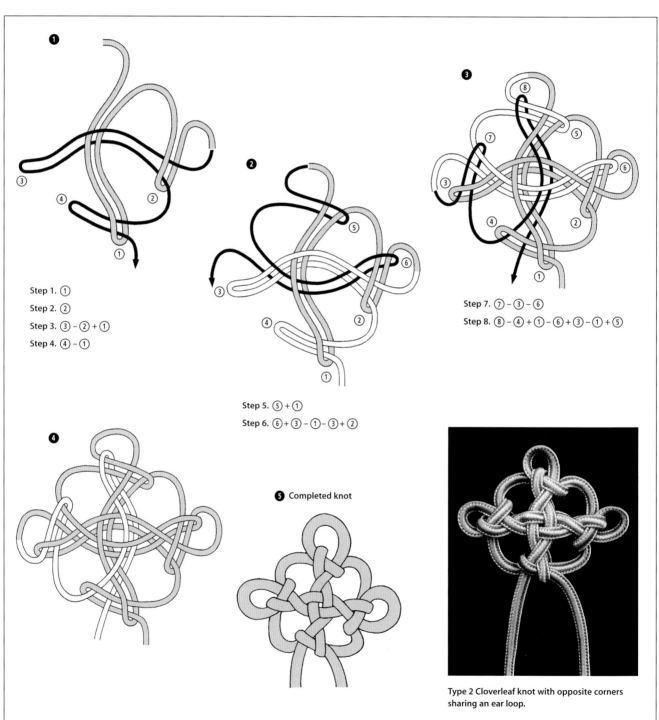

Step 1. ①
Step 2. ②
Step 3. ③ – ② + ①
Step 4. ④ – ①

Step 5. ⑤ + ①
Step 6. ⑥ + ③ – ① – ③ + ②

Step 7. ⑦ – ③ – ⑥
Step 8. ⑧ – ④ + ① – ⑥ + ③ – ① + ⑤

❺ Completed knot

Type 2 Cloverleaf knot with opposite corners sharing an ear loop.

Type 3 Cloverleaf Knot with Opposite Corners Sharing an Ear Loop

Take the curved line in opposite corners and apply the wrap two, pull two sharing technique.

TYING INSTRUCTIONS
Tie the knot following the step-by-step illustration guide below.

HINTS
See page 41.

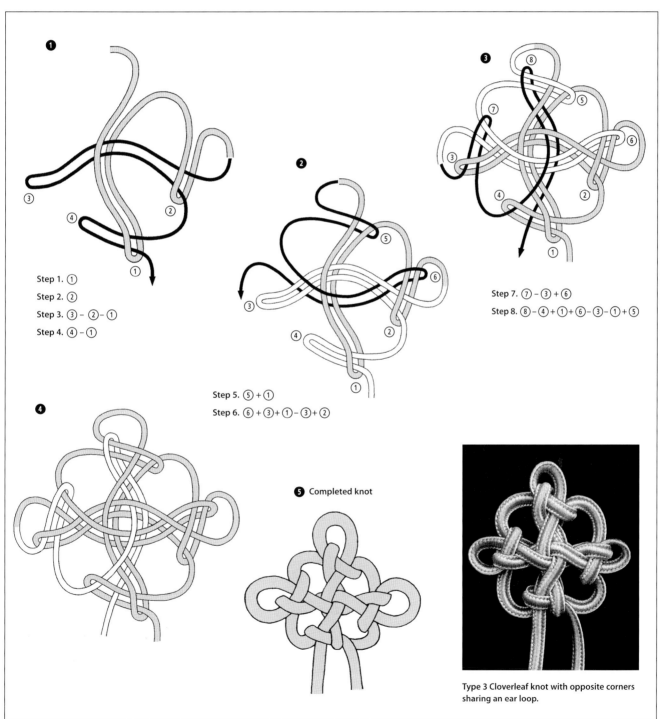

Step 1. ①
Step 2. ②
Step 3. ③ – ② – ①
Step 4. ④ – ①

Step 5. ⑤ + ①
Step 6. ⑥ + ③ + ① – ③ + ②

Step 7. ⑦ – ③ + ⑥
Step 8. ⑧ – ④ + ① + ⑥ – ③ – ① + ⑤

❺ Completed knot

Type 3 Cloverleaf knot with opposite corners sharing an ear loop.

Type 1 Cloverleaf Knot with Adjoining Sides Sharing an Ear Loop

Take the curved line in adjoining loops and apply the wrap one, pull one sharing technique.

TYING INSTRUCTIONS
Tie the knot following the step-by-step illustration guide below.

HINTS
See page 41.

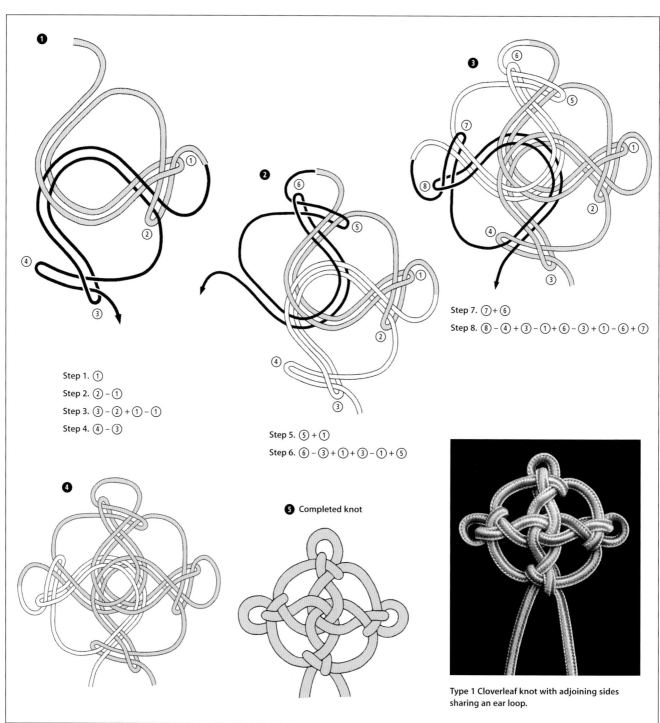

Step 1. ①

Step 2. ② – ①

Step 3. ③ – ② + ① – ①

Step 4. ④ – ③

Step 5. ⑤ + ①

Step 6. ⑥ – ③ + ① + ③ – ① + ⑤

Step 7. ⑦ + ⑥

Step 8. ⑧ – ④ + ③ – ① + ⑥ – ③ + ① – ⑥ + ⑦

❺ Completed knot

Type 1 Cloverleaf knot with adjoining sides sharing an ear loop.

Type 2(a) Cloverleaf Knot with Adjoining Sides Sharing an Ear Loop

Take the curved line in adjoining loops and apply the wrap two, pull two sharing technique.

TYING INSTRUCTIONS
Tie the knot following the step-by-step illustration guide below.

HINTS
See page 41.

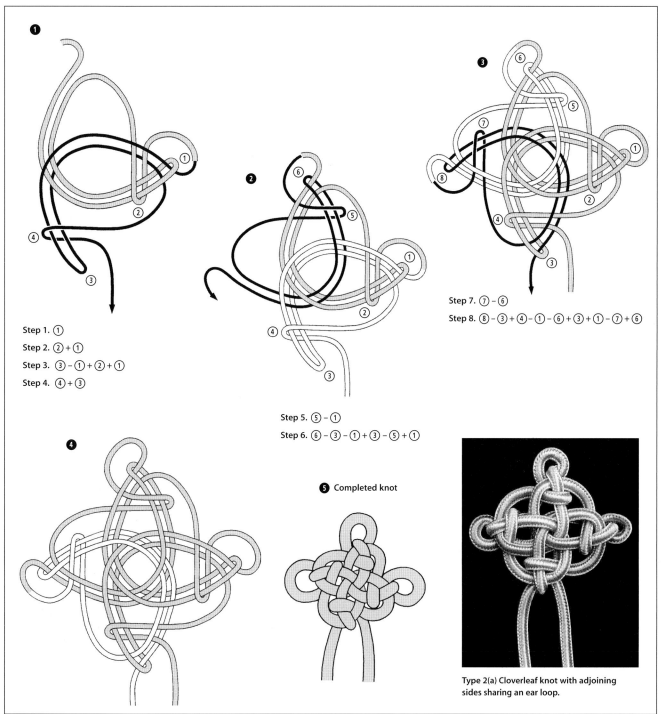

Step 1. ①
Step 2. ② + ①
Step 3. ③ − ① + ② + ①
Step 4. ④ + ③

Step 5. ⑤ − ①
Step 6. ⑥ − ③ − ① + ③ − ⑤ + ①

Step 7. ⑦ − ⑥
Step 8. ⑧ − ③ + ④ − ① − ⑥ + ③ + ① − ⑦ + ⑥

❺ Completed knot

Type 2(a) Cloverleaf knot with adjoining sides sharing an ear loop.

Type 2(b) Cloverleaf Knot with Adjoining Sides Sharing an Ear Loop

Take the curved line in adjoining loops and apply the wrap two, pull two sharing technique.

TYING INSTRUCTIONS
Tie the knot following the step-by-step illustration guide below.

HINTS
See page 41.

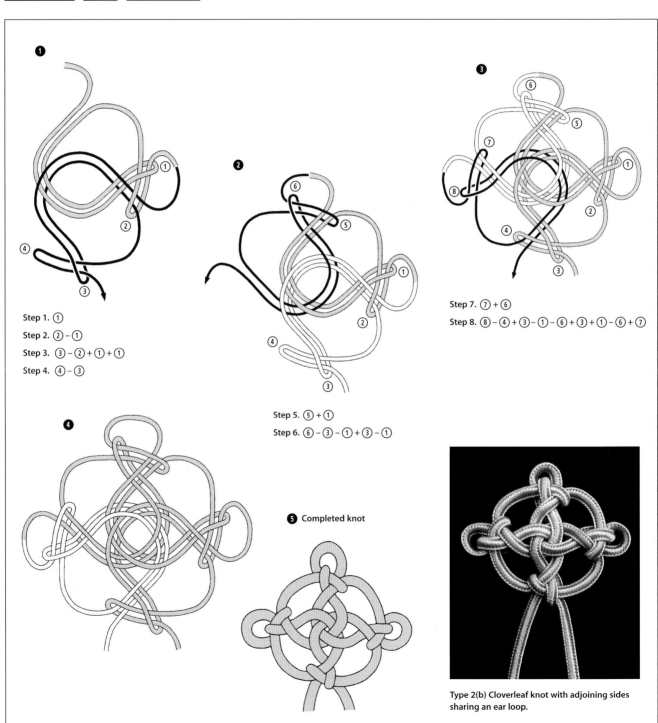

Step 1. ①
Step 2. ② – ①
Step 3. ③ – ② + ① + ①
Step 4. ④ – ③

Step 5. ⑤ + ①
Step 6. ⑥ – ③ – ① + ③ – ①

Step 7. ⑦ + ⑥
Step 8. ⑧ – ④ + ③ – ① – ⑥ + ③ + ① – ⑥ + ⑦

❺ Completed knot

Type 2(b) Cloverleaf knot with adjoining sides sharing an ear loop.

Type 3(a) Cloverleaf Knot with Adjoining Sides Sharing an Ear Loop

Take the straight line in adjoining loops and apply the sharing technique. The ear loop in the inner ring is being shared.

TYING INSTRUCTIONS
Tie the knot following the step-by-step illustration guide below.

HINTS
See page 41.

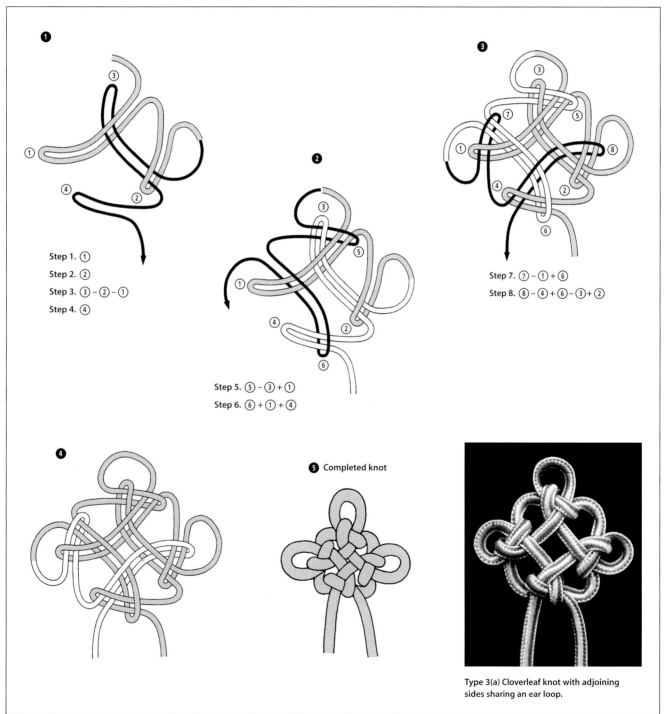

Step 1. ①
Step 2. ②
Step 3. ③ – ② – ①
Step 4. ④

Step 5. ⑤ – ③ + ①
Step 6. ⑥ + ① + ④

Step 7. ⑦ – ① + ⑥
Step 8. ⑧ – ④ + ⑥ – ③ + ②

❺ Completed knot

Type 3(a) Cloverleaf knot with adjoining sides sharing an ear loop.

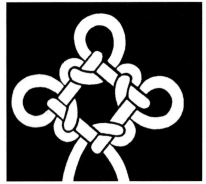

Type 3(b) Cloverleaf Knot with Adjoining Sides Sharing an Ear Loop

Take the straight line in adjoining loops and apply the sharing technique.

TYING INSTRUCTIONS
Tie the knot following the step-by-step illustration guide below.

HINTS
See page 41.

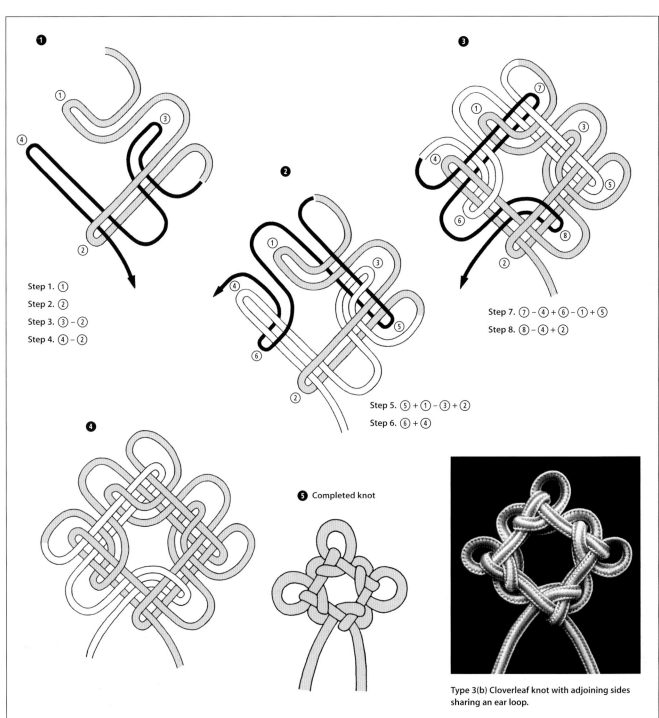

Step 1. ①
Step 2. ②
Step 3. ③ – ②
Step 4. ④ – ②

Step 5. ⑤ + ① – ③ + ②
Step 6. ⑥ + ④

Step 7. ⑦ – ④ + ⑥ – ① + ⑤
Step 8. ⑧ – ④ + ②

❺ Completed knot

Type 3(b) Cloverleaf knot with adjoining sides
sharing an ear loop.

Pan Chang Knot

In this very stable knot, the cord is woven into a double-thickness pattern. It is always tied with the outer loops on all four sides vertically down and wrapped and pulled around each other. When an ear loop of the right cord end meets another loop, it will always go through it, whereas that of the left cord end will always wrap around another loop. The last side to be completed is formed using the pull one, wrap one technique.

Modified Knots

Traditionally, the *pan chang* knot is a square knot of adjustable size. A modified *pan chang* knot is made when the shape changes despite the knotting technique remaining the same. There are four types of modified *pan chang* knots.

Solid Core Type

This includes all modified *pan chang* knots without a central hole, although the knot may be triangular, polygonal, crossed, curved or in the shape of a pagoda. All of these knots are taught in the author's second book, *Fun with Chinese Knotting: Making Your Own Fashion Accessories and Accents*.

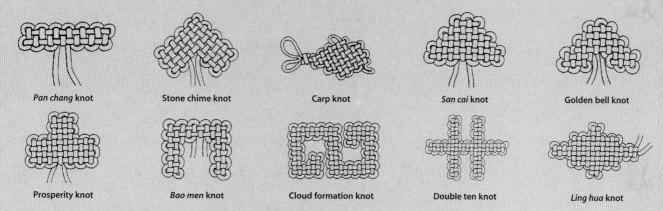

| *Pan chang* knot | Stone chime knot | Carp knot | *San cai* knot | Golden bell knot |
| Prosperity knot | *Bao men* knot | Cloud formation knot | Double ten knot | *Ling hua* knot |

Central Hole Type

Any knot with a central hole made using the *pan chang* knotting technique, regardless of whether it is square, polygonal, round, curved or in the shape of a pagoda, belongs to this group. Although the knotting technique is the same, it is important to ensure, first, that the outer loops are all linked, such as in the *ling hua* knot, and secondly, that the last side to be finished is the inner ring. If two cords are used to knot the inner and outer rings separately, always start with the peripheral knot bodies. When knotting a big knot formation, it is easier and less messy to knot with two separate cords. Again, all the knots below are taught in *Fun with Chinese Knotting*.

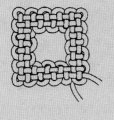
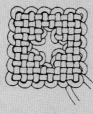

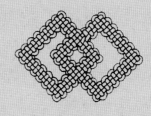

Hui ling knot   Crossed *hui ling* knot   Double *hui ling* knot   Love knot

Three-dimensional Type

The knotting process of a normal *pan chang* knot can be started in the center of the knot body, so that when the finished knot is hung, it will make a 90 degrees turn. Alternatively, some decorative side knots can be knotted on the cords in the knot body to give it a more pronounced three-dimensional effect.

Changing the Knotting Sequence of Outer Loops

This applies to *pan chang* knots with overlapped and compound outer loops.

Pan chang knot with compound outer loops.

Pan chang knot with overlapped outer loops.

Modified Knot Bodies

Shifting the Weave of the Knot Body

Here, the vertical cord, upon reaching the center of the knot body, is bent 90 degrees or 180 degrees to give a different structure to the knot body. The 90-degree change gives rise to Type 1 and the 180-degree change to Type 2 *pan chang* knots. Because the ear loops in the center of the knot body can be done in either the wrap one, pull one or wrap two, pull two technique, slightly different *pan chang* knots are produced.

Reducing the Number of Cords

When a *pan chang* knot is tied using only three sides of ear loops, the weave and structure of the knot body as well as the shape of the outer loops are changed. The resulting knot looks more like a cloverleaf knot with two outer loops and shared ear loops than a *pan chang* knot. However, since the knotting technique is that of the *pan chang* knot, this type of modified knot is called a *pan chang* knot with reduced cords.

Type 1(a) Shiftweave *pan chang* knot (see page 51).

Type 1(b) Shiftweave *pan chang* knot (see page 53).

Type 2(a) Shiftweave *pan chang* knot (see page 54).

Pan chang knot with reduced cords (see page 56).

Triangular Pan Chang Knot

The knotting technique of the *pan chang* knot is recommended for making triangular knots, for example, the *san chai* knot that is taught in *Fun with Chinese Knottting*. A diagonal weave can also be used to tie triangular knots.

Type 2(b) Shiftweave *pan chang* knot (page 55).

Triangular *pan chang* knot (see page 57).

Type 1(a) Shiftweave Pan Chang Knot

The horizontal cords in the body of a *pan chang* knot can be shifted 90 or 180 degrees to produce a modified *pan chang* knot and a modified *pan chang* good luck knot.

This modified shiftweave *pan chang* knot has a 90-degree shift, with the central weave formed using the pull one, wrap one technique. The arrangement of ear loops is the same as for the normal *pan chang* knot.

TYING INSTRUCTIONS
Step 1. Fold and arrange ear loop 1 at a 90-degree angle. **Step 2.** Pull ear loop 2 through 1. **Step 3.** Pull ear loop 3 through 2, shift it 90 degrees and wrap around 1. **Step 4.** Pull ear loop 4 through 2 and 3. **Step 5.** Wrap ear loop 5 around 1 and 2. **Step 6.** Wrap ear loop 6 around 3, shift it 90 degrees, pull through 1 and 3 and wrap around 5. **Step 7.** Pull ear loop 7 through ear loop 4 and wrap around 6 and 5. **Step 8.** Pull ear loop 8 through 4, wrap around 1, shift it 90 degrees, pull through 6, wrap around 3, pull through 1 and wrap around 7.

HINTS
• When tightening this knot, you can highlight the beauty of the central weave by adjusting the weave density on all four sides as well as the center. If you want to expand the knot, but at the same time preserve the shiftweave pattern in the center, increase the number of ear loops on each side, but make sure the number of ear loops is even.
• A *pan chang* knot with two outer loops on each side can be shifted as a group. If you want to make a multiple group shift, the number of outer loops on each side must be one plus the number of the group shift. For example, to do three group shifts, you must have four outer loops on each side of the knot.

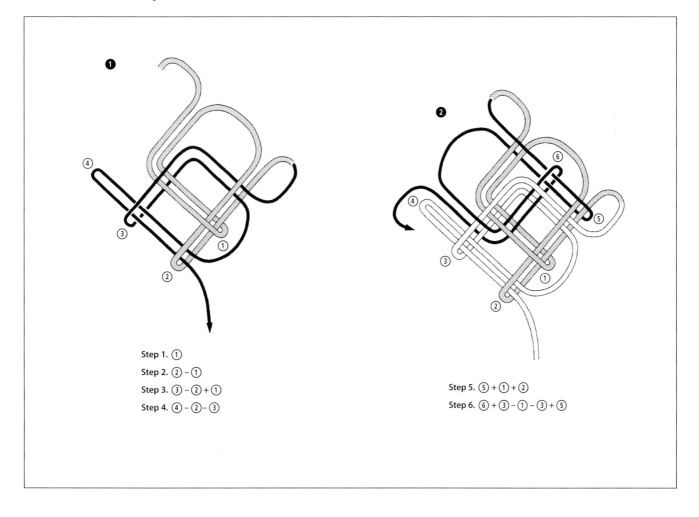

Step 1. ①
Step 2. ② – ①
Step 3. ③ – ② + ①
Step 4. ④ – ② – ③

Step 5. ⑤ + ① + ②
Step 6. ⑥ + ③ – ① – ③ + ⑤

❸

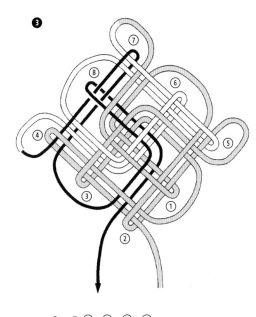

Step 7. ⑦ – ④ + ⑥ + ⑤
Step 8. ⑧ – ④ + ① – ⑥ + ③ – ① + ⑦

❹

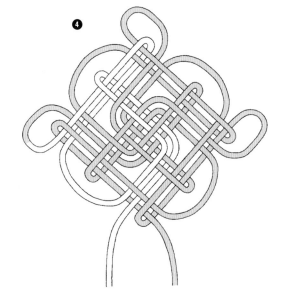

❺ Completed knot

Type 1(a) Shiftweave *pan chang* knot.

Type 1(b) Shiftweave Pan Chang Knot

This modified shiftweave *pan chang* knot has a 90-degree shift, with the central weave formed using the pull two, wrap two technique.

TYING INSTRUCTIONS
The arrangement of the ear loops is the same as for the normal *pan chang* knot.
Step 1. Fold and arrange ear loop 1 at a 90-degree angle. **Step 2.** Pull ear loop 2 through 1. **Step 3.** Pull ear loop 3 through 2, shift it 90 degrees and pull through 1. **Step 4.** Pull ear loop 4 through 2 and 3. **Step 5.** Wrap ear loop 5 around 1 and 2. **Step 6.** Wrap ear loop 6 around 3, shift it 90 degrees, wrap around 1, pull through 3 and wrap around 5. **Step 7.** Pull ear loop 7 through 4 and wrap around 6 and 5. **Step 8.** Pull ear loop 8 through 4, wrap around 1, shift it 90 degrees, wrap around 6, pull through 3 and 1 and wrap around 7.

HINTS
See page 51.

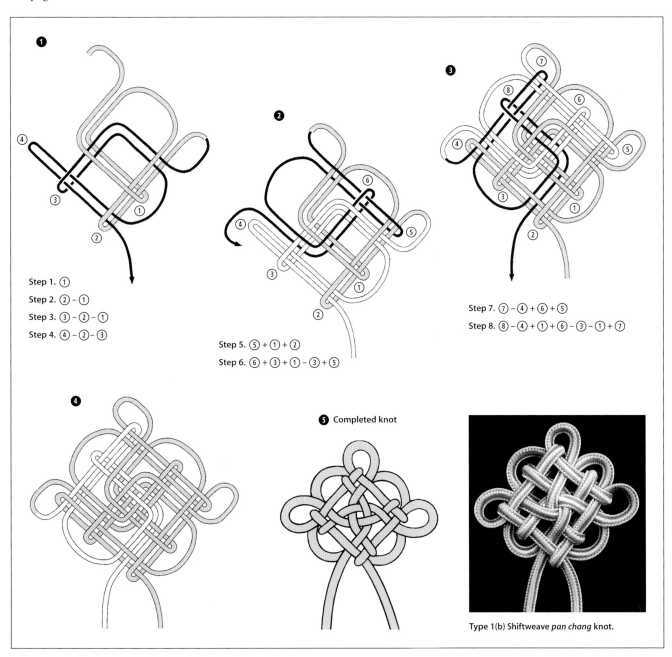

Step 1. ①
Step 2. ② – ①
Step 3. ③ – ② – ①
Step 4. ④ – ② – ③

Step 5. ⑤ + ① + ②
Step 6. ⑥ + ③ + ① – ③ + ⑤

Step 7. ⑦ – ④ + ⑥ + ⑤
Step 8. ⑧ – ④ + ① + ⑥ – ③ – ① + ⑦

❺ Completed knot

Type 1(b) Shiftweave *pan chang* knot.

Type 2(a) Shiftweave Pan Chang Knot

This modified *pan chang* knot has a 180-degree shift, with the central weave formed using the wrap one, pull one technique.

TYING INSTRUCTIONS

The arrangement of the ear loops is the same as for the normal *pan chang* knot. **Step 1.** Fold and arrange ear loop 1 at a 180-degree angle. **Step 2.** Ear loop 2 follows the same angle. **Step 3.** Pull ear loop 3 through 2, wrap around 1, shift it 180 degrees, pull through 1 and wrap around 2. **Step 4.** Pull ear loop 4 through 2. **Step 5.** Wrap ear loop 5 around 1, pull through 1 and wrap around 2. **Step 6.** Pull ear loop 6 through 3, shift it 180 degrees, wrap around 1 and 3 and pull through 1. **Step 7.** Pull ear loop 7 through 4, wrap around 6, pull through 6 and wrap around 5. **Step 8.** Pull ear loop 8 through 4, wrap around 3, pull through 1, shift it 180 degress, wrap around 6, pull through 3, wrap around 1, pull through 6 and wrap around 4.

HINTS
See page 51.

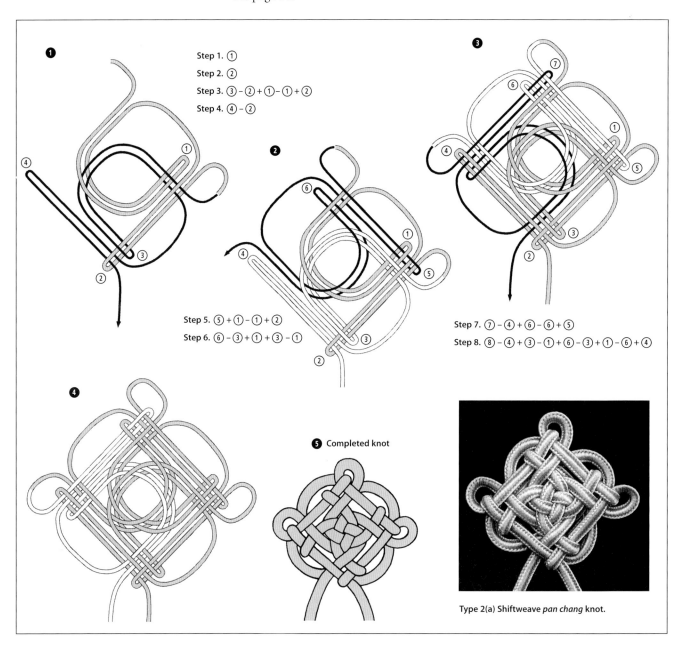

Step 1. ①
Step 2. ②
Step 3. ③ – ② + ① – ① + ②
Step 4. ④ – ②

Step 5. ⑤ + ① – ① + ②
Step 6. ⑥ – ③ + ① + ③ – ①

Step 7. ⑦ – ④ + ⑥ – ⑥ + ⑤
Step 8. ⑧ – ④ + ③ – ① + ⑥ – ③ + ① – ⑥ + ④

❺ Completed knot

Type 2(a) Shiftweave *pan chang* knot.

Type 2(b) Shiftweave Pan Chang Knot

This modified *pan chang* knot has a 180-degree shift, with the central weave formed using the pull two, wrap two technique.

TYING INSTRUCTIONS
The arrangement of the ear loops is the same as for the normal *pan chang* knot. **Step 1.** Fold and arrange ear loop 1 at a 180-degree angle. **Step 2.** Ear loop 2 follows the same angle. **Step 3.** Pull ear loop 3 through 2, wrap around 1, shift it 180 degrees and wrap around 1 and 2. **Step 4.** Pull ear loop 4 through 2. **Step 5.** Wrap ear loop 5 around 1, pull through 1 and wrap around 2. **Step 6.** Pull ear loop 6 through 3, shift it 180 degrees, pull through 1, wrap around 3 and pull through 1. **Step 7.** Pull ear loop 7 through 4, wrap around 6, pull through 6 and wrap around 5. **Step 8.** Pull ear loop 8 through 4, wrap around 3, shift it 180 degrees, pull through 1 and 6, wrap around 3 and 1, pull through 6 and wrap around 4.

HINTS
See page 51.

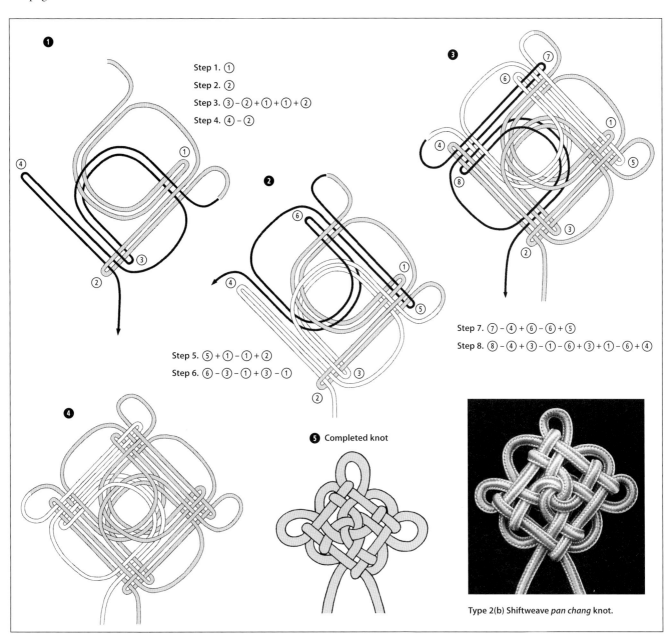

5 Completed knot

Type 2(b) Shiftweave *pan chang* knot.

Pan Chang Knot with Reduced Cords

This modified *pan chang* knot has three ear loops on each side.

TYING INSTRUCTIONS

Steps 1–3. Employing the knotting technique of the *pan chang* knot, use the left cord end to arrange ear loops 1, 2 and 3 in straight lines. **Steps 4–6.** Use the left cord end to knot ear loops 4, 5 and 6 using the wrapping technique. **Steps 7–11.** For the last side, use the left cord to knot ear loops 7, 8, 9, 10 and 11 by the pull one, wrap one technique.

HINTS

• If you want to tie a reduced cord *pan chang* knot into an irregular shape, arrange the desired shape straight away when doing the first side.
• During the tightening process, you can adjust the knot body weave in three different ways to achieve the particular design you want.

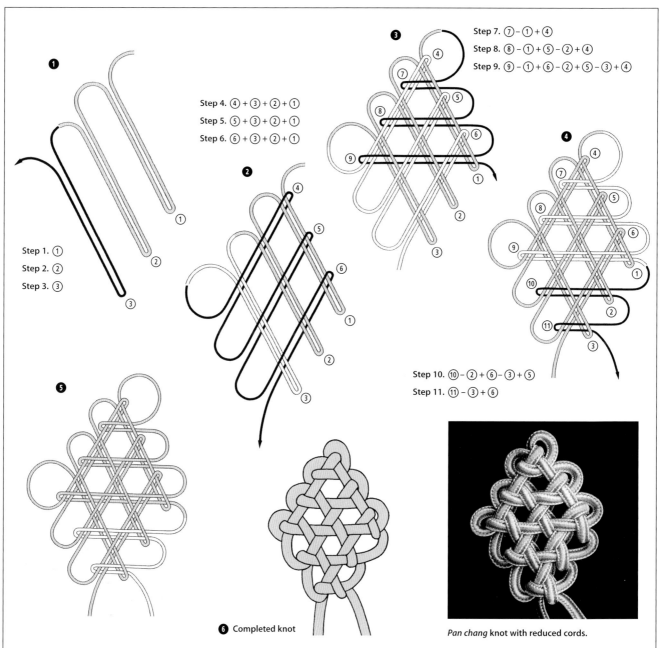

Step 1. ①
Step 2. ②
Step 3. ③

Step 4. ④ + ③ + ② + ①
Step 5. ⑤ + ③ + ② + ①
Step 6. ⑥ + ③ + ② + ①

Step 7. ⑦ - ① + ④
Step 8. ⑧ - ① + ⑤ - ② + ④
Step 9. ⑨ - ① + ⑥ - ② + ⑤ - ③ + ④

Step 10. ⑩ - ② + ⑥ - ③ + ⑤
Step 11. ⑪ - ③ + ⑥

❻ Completed knot

Pan chang knot with reduced cords.

Triangular Pan Chang Knot

This modified *pan chang* knot has two ear loops on each side.

TYING INSTRUCTIONS
Steps 1, 2. Employing the knotting technique of the *pan chang* knot, use the right cord end to arrange ear loops 1 and 2 using the pulling technique. **Steps 3, 4.** Use the left cord end to arrange ear loops 3 and 4 using the wrapping technique. **Steps 5, 6.** For the last side, use the left cord end (or both cord ends simultaneously) to knot ear loops 5 and 6 using the pull one, wrap one technique.

HINT
You can use either a single cord end or both cord ends to finish the knot according to the design and application that you want to achieve.

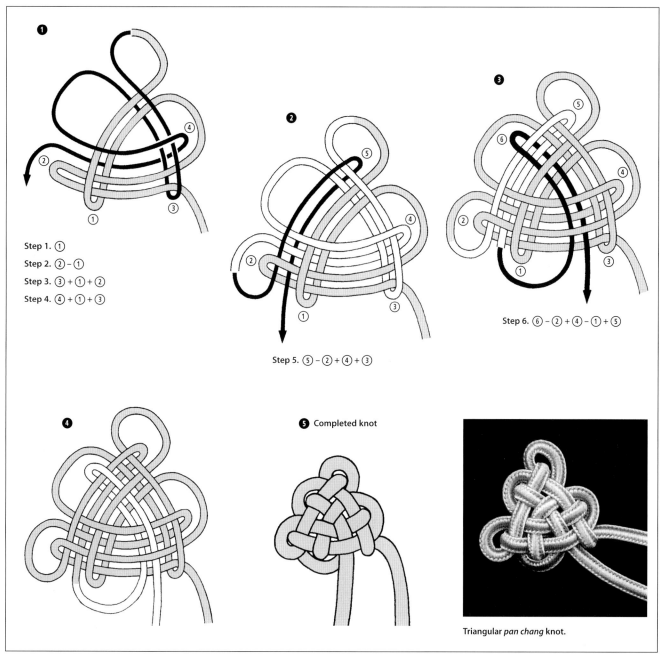

❶

Step 1. ①
Step 2. ② – ①
Step 3. ③ + ① + ②
Step 4. ④ + ① + ③

❷

Step 5. ⑤ – ② + ④ + ③

❸

Step 6. ⑥ – ② + ④ – ① + ⑤

❹

❺ Completed knot

Triangular *pan chang* knot.

Round Brocade Knot

The round brocade knot was developed to rectify the shortcomings of the cloverleaf knot with multiple outer loops, which has a loose body knot and a lack of variety in its modifications. As with the *pan chang* knot, the basic round brocade knot uses the pull and wrap technique. Though the *pan chang* knot is squarish and the round brocade knot round, as its name suggests, both knots are highly versatile and variable. The different types of modified round brocade knots are shown below.

Modified Knots

Increasing the Number of Outer Loops

In theory, an infinite number of outer loops can be added to the round brocade knot. However, when there are too many outer loops, the central hole tends to become too big and the knot body too loose. This is fine if you want this kind of modified knot to take the form of a big decorative ring. To make the central hole smaller, instead of looping every second outer loop, you can loop every third or fourth. But in this case, it would become a fairly thick knot.

Round brocade knot with multiple outer loops.

Changing the Knotting Sequence of Outer Loops

The round brocade knot can be tied with both compound and overlapped outer loops. Since the number of outer loops can be increased indefinitely, the number of variations is also large.

Round brocade knot with compound outer loops (see page 59).

Round brocade knot with overlapped outer loops (see page 61).

Modified Knot Bodies

Varying the Ear Loops

The basic knotting technique of the round brocade knot can be changed by extending the ear loops, thereby increasing the number of pulls and wraps.

Compound round brocade knot (see page 63).

Round Brocade Knot with Compound Outer Loops

The technique used for this modified knot is the same as for the basic round brocade knot except that the knotting sequence of some of the ear loops is reversed, i.e. those with bigger numbers have to be knotted first and those with smaller numbers last. The same applies to the round brocade knot with overlapped outer loops described on pages 61–2.

Before beginning the compound knot, it is necessary first of all to determine and calculate the number of overlapped or repeated outer loops you want to include, as well as the total number of ear loops involved. The butterfly knot with overlapped outer loops shown here is done by wrapping the tenth and fourth ear loops.

TYING INSTRUCTIONS

Step 1. Make ear loop 1. **Step 2.** Pull ear loop 3 through 1. **Step 3.** Pull ear loop 4 through 1 and 3. **Step 4.** Turn back the cord end to make ear loop 2, pull through 1 and wrap around 3 and 4. **Step 5.** Make ear loop 5 and pull through 1, 2, 3 and 4. **Step 6.** Pull ear loop 6 through 2, 3, 4 and 5. **Step 7.** Make ear loop 9 and pull through 5 and 6 and wrap around 1, 2 and 3. **Step 8.** Make ear loop 7, pull through 3, 4, 5 and 6 and wrap around 9 and 1. **Step 9.** Pull ear loop 8 through 4, 5, 6 and 7 and wrap around 9, 1 and 2. **Step 10.** Pull ear loop 10 through 6, 7, 8 and 9 and wrap around 1, 2, 3 and 4.

HINTS

• When making a round brocade knot with compound/overlapped outer loops, remember that the knotting sequence of some of the ear loops must be reversed. For example, when a front ear loop (i.e. one with a smaller number) meets a subsequent ear loop (i.e. one with a bigger number), it must always be wrapped around the latter.

• Before tightening the knot, adjust the outer loops of the compound/overlapped arrangements so that the left and right sides are identical for optimal aesthetic effect.

• During the final stage of knotting such a knot with x number of ear loops, the last ear loop must not only loop the number of ear loops it is supposed to loop, but also the first loop in the knotting process. For example, if you want to tie a knot that is looped every fourth ear loop, during the final stage you must count backwards to tie the fourth last ear loop, loop four ear loops with it, and then loop the first loop in the entire knotting process. Subsequently, you must tie the third last ear loop, loop four ear loops with it, then loop the second loop in the entire knotting process and so on.

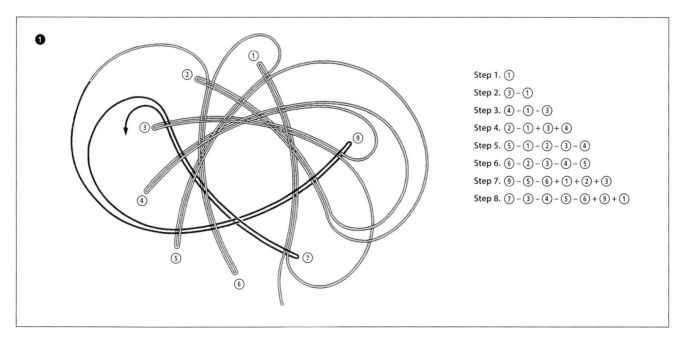

Step 1. ①
Step 2. ③ - ①
Step 3. ④ - ① - ③
Step 4. ② - ① + ③ + ④
Step 5. ⑤ - ① - ② - ③ - ④
Step 6. ⑥ - ② - ③ - ④ - ⑤
Step 7. ⑨ - ⑤ - ⑥ + ① + ② + ③
Step 8. ⑦ - ③ - ④ - ⑤ - ⑥ + ⑨ + ①

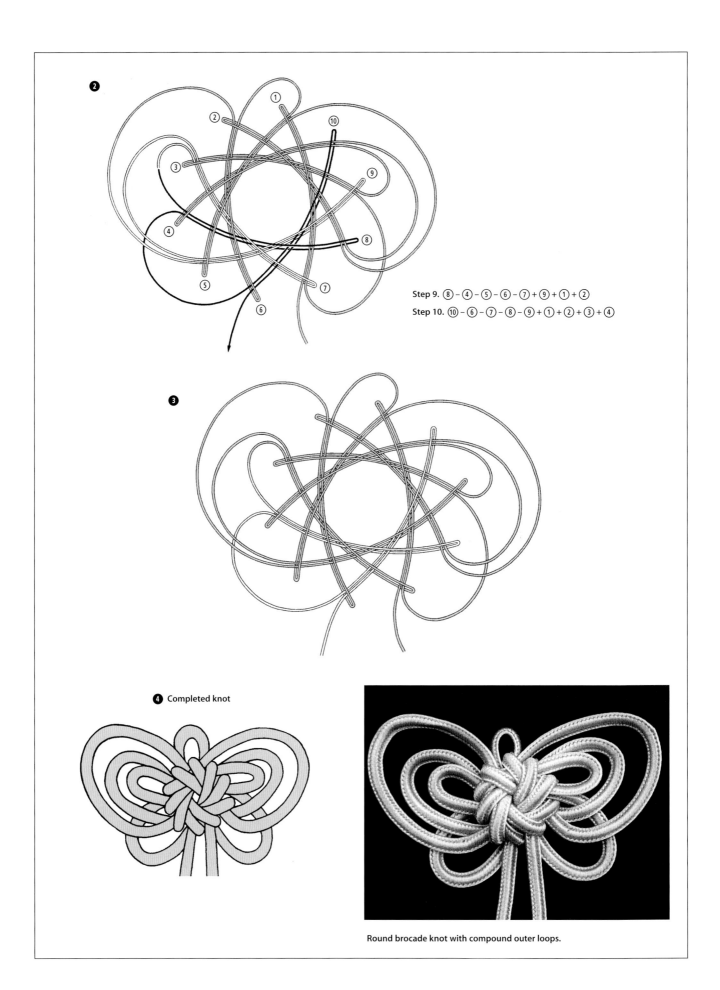

Step 9. ⑧ − ④ − ⑤ − ⑥ − ⑦ + ⑨ + ① + ②

Step 10. ⑩ − ⑥ − ⑦ − ⑧ − ⑨ + ① + ② + ③ + ④

❹ Completed knot

Round brocade knot with compound outer loops.

Round Brocade Knot with Overlapped Outer Loops

The knotting technique of this modified knot is the same as for the round brocade knot with compound outer loops (pages 59–60) except that the knotting sequence of certain ear loops is changed in order to emphasize the overlapped loops. The butterfly knot with overlapped outer loops shown here is done by wrapping the tenth and fourth ear loops.

TYING INSTRUCTIONS
Step 1. Make ear loop 1. **Step 2.** Make ear loop 3 and pull through 1. **Step 3.** Make ear loop 2, pull through 1 and wrap around 3. **Step 4.** Make ear loop 4 and pull through 1, 2 and 3. **Step 5.** Make ear loop 5 and pull through 1, 2, 3 and 4. **Step 6.** Make ear loop 6 and pull through 2, 3, 4 and 5. **Step 7.** Make ear loop 7, pull through 3, 4, 5 and 6 and wrap around 1. **Step 8.** Make ear loop 9, pull through 5, 6 and 7 and wrap around 1, 2 and 3. **Step 9.** Make ear loop 8, pull through 4, 5, 6 and 7 and wrap around 9, 1 and 2. **Step 10.** Make ear loop 10, pull through 6, 7, 8 and 9 and wrap around 1, 2, 3 and 4.

HINTS
See page 59.

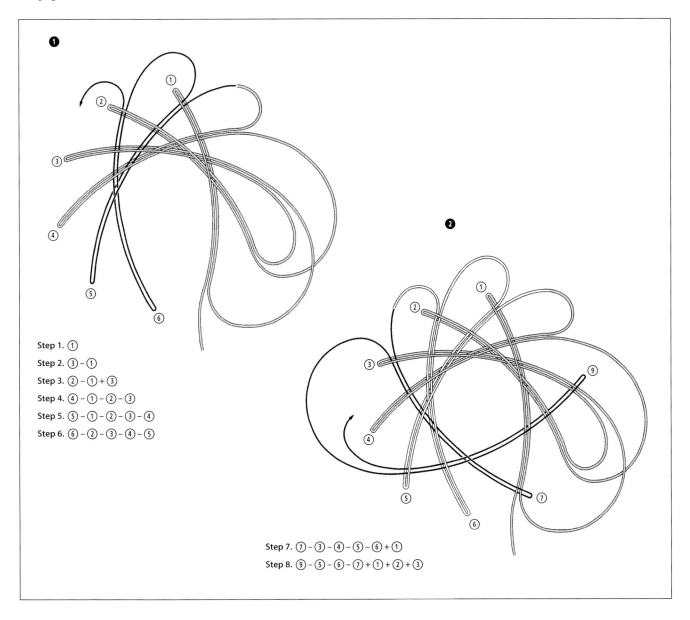

Step 1. ①
Step 2. ③ – ①
Step 3. ② – ① + ③
Step 4. ④ – ① – ② – ③
Step 5. ⑤ – ① – ② – ③ – ④
Step 6. ⑥ – ② – ③ – ④ – ⑤

Step 7. ⑦ – ③ – ④ – ⑤ – ⑥ + ①
Step 8. ⑨ – ⑤ – ⑥ – ⑦ + ① + ② + ③

Step 9. ⑧ − ④ − ⑤ − ⑥ − ⑦ + ⑨ + ① + ②

Step 10. ⑩ − ⑥ − ⑦ − ⑧ − ⑨ + ① + ② + ③ + ④

5 Completed knot

Round brocade knot with overlapped outer loops.

Compound Round Brocade Knot

This modified knot shares the same knotting technique as the compound cloverleaf knot, i.e. the ear loops of the basic round brocade knot are extended and the number of wraps and pulls increased. The basic round brocade knot can be turned into one with six outer loops by applying the pull one, wrap one technique on the ear loops.

TYING INSTRUCTIONS
Step 1. Make ear loop 1. **Step 2.** Make ear loop 2 and pull through 1. **Step 3.** Make ear loop 3, pull through 1 and 2 and wrap around 1. **Step 4.** Make ear loop 4, wrap around 1, pull through 2, 3 and 1 and wrap around 2. **Step 5.** Make ear loop 5, pull through 1, wrap around 2, pull through 3 and 4, wrap around 1, pull through 2 and wrap around 3. **Step 6.** Make ear loop 6, pull through 2, wrap around 3, pull through 4 and 5, wrap around 1 and 2, pull through 3 and wrap around 4.

Use the formula application on page 64 to tie this type of compound brocade knot with multiple outer loops.

HINT
It is quite difficult to adjust and tighten the ear loops in this knot body because of the many pulls and wraps involved. Hence, it is necessary to adjust and standardize the curvature of each curving ear loop to achieve optimal aesthetic effect.

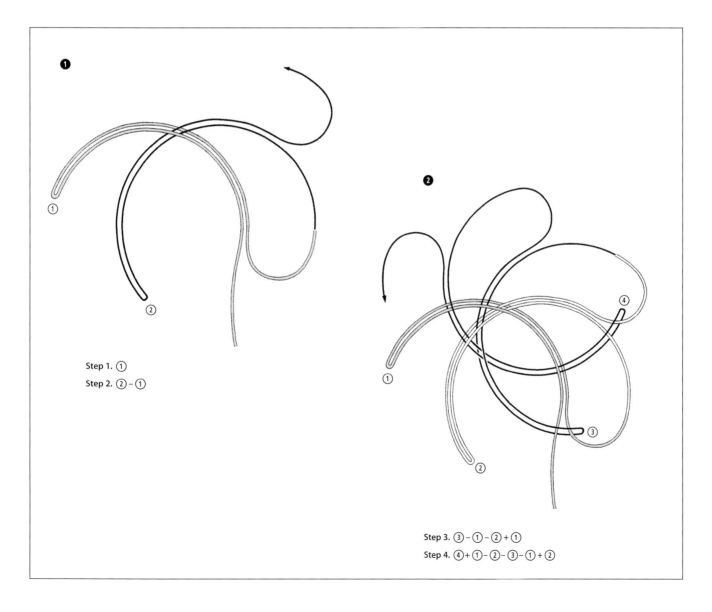

Step 1. ①
Step 2. ② – ①

Step 3. ③ – ① – ② + ①
Step 4. ④ + ① – ② – ③ – ① + ②

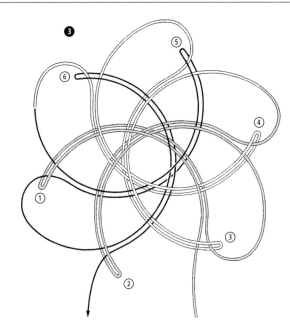

❸

Step 5. ⑤ − ① + ② − ③ − ④ + ① − ② + ③

Step 6. ⑥ − ② + ③ − ④ − ⑤ + ① + ② − ③ + ④

❹

❺ Completed knot

Formula for compound round brocade knots with multiple outer loops:
a. (x) − (x−4) + (x−3) − (x−2) − (x−1)
b. (n−3) − (n−3−4) + (n−3−3) − (n−3−2) − (n−3−1) + ①
   (n−2) − (n−2−4) + (n−2−3) − (n−2−2) − (n−2−1) − ① + ②
   (n−1) − (n−1−4) + (n−1−3) − (n−1−2) − (n−1−1) + ① − ② + ③
   (n) − (n−4) + (n−3) − (n−2) − (n−1) + ① + ② − ③ + ④

Formula application:
1. "x" denotes the number of each ear loop.
   "n" denotes the total number of ear loops; "n" is larger than 4.
2. When the value of "x" is not enough for subtraction, then that item does not exist.
   Example: x = 3 and insert this into the equation to give
       ③ − ① − ②
       x = 5 and insert this into the equation to give
       ⑤ − ① + ② − ③ − ④
3. Use formula "a" for all ear loops except the number 4 by counting backwards. Use formula "b" for this particular ear loop.

Compound round brocade knot.

Constellation Knot

This knot, tied using the wrap one, pull one technique, resembles a star, hence its name. By varying the number of ear loops and their sequence, a series of modified constellation knots can be produced, although fairly similar in appearance.

Modified Knots

Increasing the Number of Ear Loops

Using the knotting technique of the basic constellation knot, the number of ear loops can be increased, for example to 4, 5, 6, etc., to produce knots with a varying number of outer loops. As with the round brocade knot, however, the more outer loops there are, the larger the central hole becomes. This can be remedied by wrapping every second or third ear loop, etc. instead of every one. In this way, the central hole will become smaller although the knot itself will be thicker.

Constellation knot with four outer loops (see page 66).

Constellation knot with five outer loops (see page 67).

Changing the Knotting Sequence of Ear Loops

The constellation knot can be tied with both compound and overlapped outer loops. Since the number of outer loops can be increased indefinitely, the number of variations is also large.

Constellation knot with compound outer loops (see page 69).

Constellation knot with overlapped outer loops (see page 71).

Modified Knot Bodies

The basic knotting technique of the constellation knot can be changed by extending the ear loops, thereby increasing the number of pulls and wraps. Similarly, by varying the wrap and pull technique of the knot body weave, four types of compound constellation knots are possible.

Varying and Extending Ear Loops

Type 1 Compound constellation knot (see page 73).

Type 2 Compound constellation knot (see page 75).

Type 3 Compound constellation knot (see page 77).

Type 4 Compound constellation knot (see page 79).

Constellation Knot with Four Outer Loops

The simplest constellation knot is tied using the pull one, wrap one technique. This knot, with five ear loops and four outer loops, most resembles a star in the sky.

TYING INSTRUCTIONS
Step 1. Make ear loop 1. **Step 2.** Make ear loop 2 and wrap around 1. **Step 3.** Make ear loop 3, pull through 1 and wrap around 2. **Step 4.** Make ear loop 4, pull through 2 and wrap around 3 and 1. **Step 5.** Make ear loop 5, pull through 3, wrap around 4, pull through 1 and wrap around 2.

Use the formula application below to tie a constellation knot with multiple outer loops.

HINT
Since most parts of the knot body are exposed, make sure that the curvature of each ear loop is the same for optimal aesthetic effect.

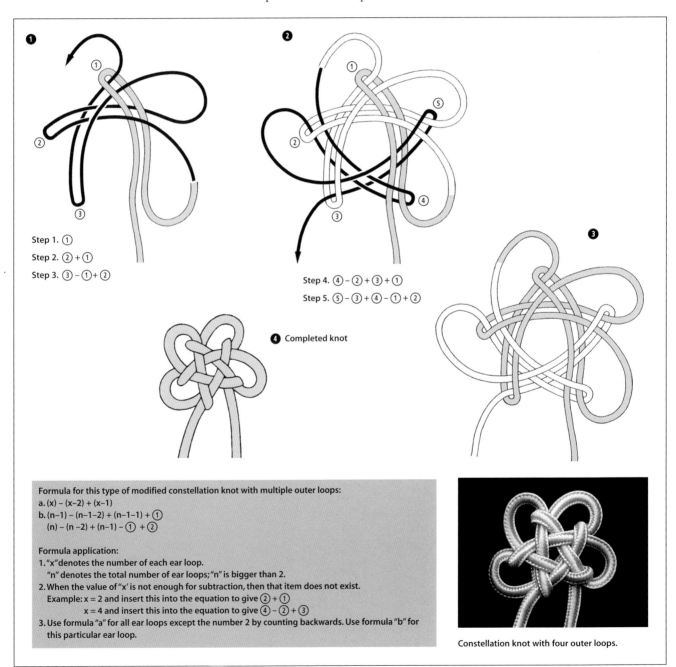

❶

Step 1. ①
Step 2. ② + ①
Step 3. ③ − ① + ②

❷

Step 4. ④ − ② + ③ + ①
Step 5. ⑤ − ③ + ④ − ① + ②

❹ Completed knot

❸

Formula for this type of modified constellation knot with multiple outer loops:
a. (x) − (x−2) + (x−1)
b. (n−1) − (n−1−2) + (n−1−1) + ①
   (n) − (n −2) + (n−1) − ① + ②

Formula application:
1. "x" denotes the number of each ear loop.
   "n" denotes the total number of ear loops; "n" is bigger than 2.
2. When the value of "x" is not enough for subtraction, then that item does not exist.
   Example: x = 2 and insert this into the equation to give ② + ①
            x = 4 and insert this into the equation to give ④ − ② + ③
3. Use formula "a" for all ear loops except the number 2 by counting backwards. Use formula "b" for this particular ear loop.

Constellation knot with four outer loops.

Constellation Knot with Five Outer Loops

This is made from a basic constellation knot using the technique of wrapping every second ear loop. The same technique can be used to make constellation knots with six, seven or more outer loops.

TYING INSTRUCTIONS
1. Tie the knot following the step-by-step illustration guide below.
2. Use the formula application on page 68 to tie a constellation knot with "n" number of outer loops.

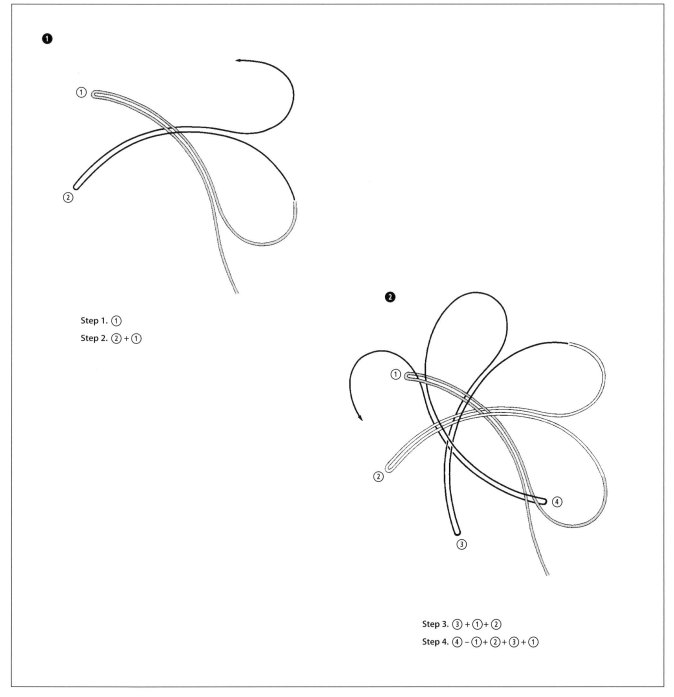

Step 1. ①
Step 2. ② + ①

Step 3. ③ + ① + ②
Step 4. ④ − ① + ② + ③ + ①

❸

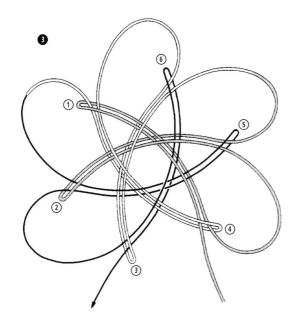

Step 5. ⑤ − ② + ③ + ④ − ① + ②

Step 6. ⑥ − ③ + ④ + ⑤ − ① − ② + ③

❹

❺ Completed knot

Formula for this type of modified constellation knot with multiple outer loops:
a. (x) − (x−3) + (x−2) + (x−1)
b. (n−2) − (n−2−3) + (n−2−2) + (n−2−1) + ①
   (n−1) − (n−1−3) + (n−1−2) + (n−1−1) − ① + ②
   (n) − (n−3) + (n−2) + (n−1) − ① − ② + ③

Formula application:
1. "x" denotes the number of each ear loop.
   "n" denotes the total number of ear loops; "n" is bigger than 3.
2. When the value of "x" is not enough for subtraction, then that item does not exist.
   Example x = 3 and insert this into the equation to give ③ + ① + ②
       x = 5 and insert this into he equation to give ⑤ − ② + ③ + ④
3. Use formula "a" for all ear loops except to number 3 by counting backwards.
   Use formula "b" for this particular ear loop.

Constellation knot with five outer loops.

Constellation Knot with Compound Outer Loops

This modified knot shares the same knotting technique as the constellation knot except that the knotting sequence of certain ear loops is changed, as in the case of the round brocade knot with compound outer loops (page 59). The butterfly knot with compound outer loops shown here is made by wrapping the tenth and fourth ear loops.

TYING INSTRUCTIONS
Step 1. Make ear loop 1. **Step 2.** Make ear loop 3 and wrap around 1. **Step 3.** Make ear loop 4 and wrap around 1 and 3. **Step 4.** Turn back the cord end to make ear loop 2, wrap around 1 and pull through 3 and 4. **Step 5.** Make ear loop 5 and wrap around 1, 2, 3 and 4. **Step 6.** Make ear loop 6, pull through 1 and wrap around 2, 3, 4, 5 and 1. **Step 7.** Make ear loop 9, pull through 4, wrap around 5 and 6, pull through 1, 2 and 3 and wrap around 4. **Step 8.** Make ear loop 7, pull through 2, wrap around 3, 4, 5 and 6, pull through 9 and 1 and wrap around 2. **Step 9.** Make ear loop 8, pull through 3, wrap around 4, 5, 6, and 7, pull through 9, 1 and 2 and wrap around 3. **Step 10.** Make ear loop 10, pull through 5, wrap around 6, 7, 8 and 9, pull through 1, 2, 3 and 4 and wrap around 5.

HINT
During the tightening process, make sure that both sides and the curvature of each ear loop are identical.

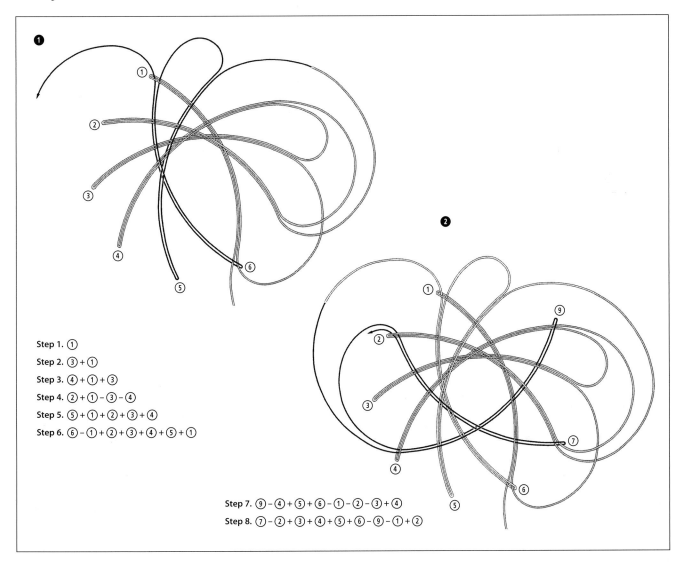

Step 1. ①
Step 2. ③ + ①
Step 3. ④ + ① + ③
Step 4. ② + ① − ③ − ④
Step 5. ⑤ + ① + ② + ③ + ④
Step 6. ⑥ − ① + ② + ③ + ④ + ⑤ + ①

Step 7. ⑨ − ④ + ⑤ + ⑥ − ① − ② − ③ + ④
Step 8. ⑦ − ② + ③ + ④ + ⑤ + ⑥ − ⑨ − ① + ②

❸

Step 9. ⑧ − ③ + ④ + ⑤ + ⑥ + ⑦ − ⑨ − ① − ② + ③

Step 10. ⑩ − ⑤ + ⑥ + ⑦ + ⑧ + ⑨ − ① − ② − ③ − ④ + ⑤

❹

❺ Completed knot

Constellation knot with compound outer loops.

Constellation Knot with Overlapped Outer Loops

The constellation knot with overlapped outer loops shares the same knotting technique as that with compound outer loops except that the knotting sequence of certain ear loops is changed. The butterfly knot with overlapped outer loops shown here is done by wrapping the tenth and fourth ear loops.

TYING INSTRUCTIONS

Step 1. Make ear loop 1. **Step 2**. Make ear loop 3 and wrap around 1. **Step 3**. Make ear loop 2, wrap around 1 and pull through 3. **Step 4**. Make ear loop 4 and wrap around 1, 2 and 3. **Step 5**. Make ear loop 5 and wrap around 1, 2, 3 and 4. **Step 6**. Make ear loop 6, pull through 1 and wrap around 2, 3, 4, 5 and 1. **Step 7**. Make ear loop 7, pull through 2, wrap around 3, 4, 5 and 6, pull through 1 and wrap around 2. **Step 8**. Make ear loop 9, pull through 4, wrap around 5, 6 and 7, pull through 1, 2 and 3 and wrap around 4. **Step 9**. Make ear loop 8, pull through 3, wrap around 4, 5, 6 and 7, pull through 9, 1 and 2 and wrap around 3. **Step 10**. Make ear loop 10, pull through 5, wrap around 6, 7, 8 and 9, pull through 1, 2, 3 and 4 and wrap around 5.

HINT
See page 69.

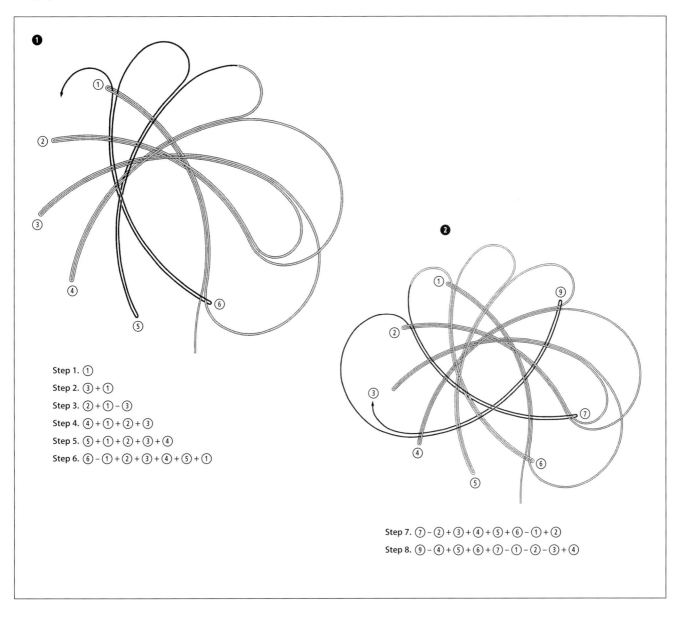

Step 1. ①
Step 2. ③ + ①
Step 3. ② + ① – ③
Step 4. ④ + ① + ② + ③
Step 5. ⑤ + ① + ② + ③ + ④
Step 6. ⑥ – ① + ② + ③ + ④ + ⑤ + ①

Step 7. ⑦ – ② + ③ + ④ + ⑤ + ⑥ – ① + ②
Step 8. ⑨ – ④ + ⑤ + ⑥ + ⑦ – ① – ② – ③ + ④

3

Step 9. ⑧ − ③ + ④ + ⑤ + ⑥ + ⑦ − ⑨ − ① − ② + ③
Step 10. ⑩ − ⑤ + ⑥ + ⑦ + ⑧ + ⑨ − ① − ② − ③ − ④ + ⑤

4

5 Completed knot

Constellation knot with overlapped outer loops.

Type 1 Compound Constellation Knot

When a constellation knot is tied with multiple outer loops, the same problem occurs as with the round brocade knot with multiple outer loops, i.e. the more outer loops there are, the bigger the central hole. The remedy, besides wrapping a larger number of ear loops every time, includes extending the ear loops as well as increasing the number of pulls and wraps, as recommended for the various compound cloverleaf knots and compound round brocade knots.

The Type 1 Compound constellation knot is formed using the one loop, one wrap technique to tie five outer loops.

TYING INSTRUCTIONS
Step 1. Make ear loop 1. **Step 2.** Make ear loop 2 and wrap around 1. **Step 3.** Make ear loop 3, pull through 1 and wrap around 2 and 1. **Step 4.** Make ear loop 4, wrap around 1, pull through 2, wrap around 3, pull through 1 and wrap around 2. **Step 5.** Make ear loop 5, pull through 1, wrap around 2, pull through 3, wrap around 4 and 1, pull through 2 and wrap around 3. **Step 6.** Make ear loop 6, pull through 2, wrap around 3, pull through 4, wrap around 5, pull through 1, wrap around 2, pull through 3 and wrap around 4.

Use the formula application on page 74 to tie a compound constellation knot with multiple outer loops.

HINT
Since there are many pulls and wraps involved here, it is quite difficult to tighten and adjust the knot. Make sure you adjust each ear loop to the same curvature for optimal aesthetic effect.

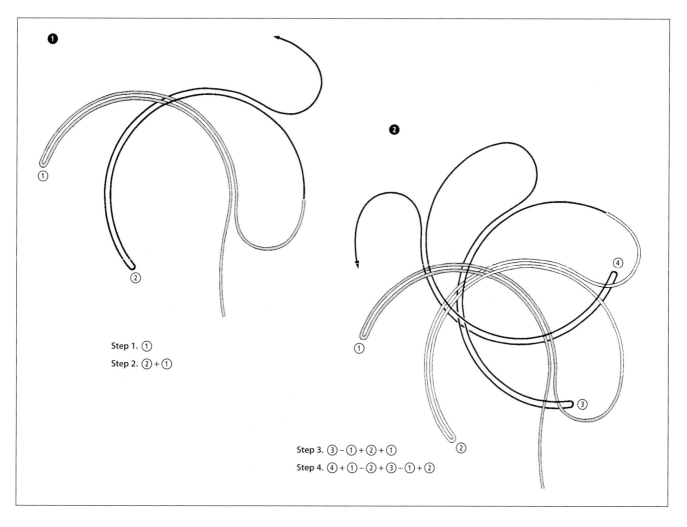

Step 1. ①
Step 2. ② + ①

Step 3. ③ − ① + ② + ①
Step 4. ④ + ① − ② + ③ − ① + ②

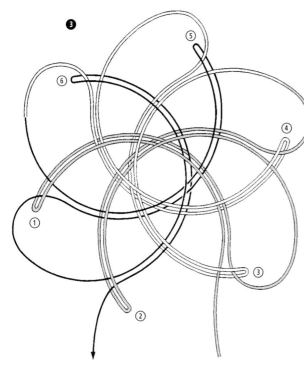

❸

Step 5. ⑤ – ① + ② – ③ + ④ + ① – ② + ③

Step 6. ⑥ – ② + ③ – ④ + ⑤ – ① + ② – ③ + ④

❹

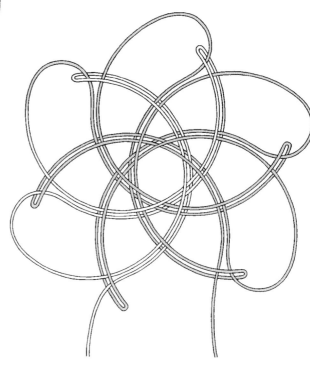

❺ Completed knot

Formula for Type 1 Compound constellation knot with multiple outer loops:

a. (x) – (x–4) + (x–3) – (x–2) + (x–1)

b. (n–3) – (n–3–4) + (n–3–3) – (n–3–2) + (n–3–1) + ①
(n–2) – (n–2–4) + (n–2–3) – (n–2–2) + (n–2–1) – ① + ②
(n–1) – (n–1–4) + (n–1–3) – (n–1–2) + (n–1–1) + ① – ② + ③
(n) – (n–4) + (n–3) – (n–2) + (n–1) – ① + ② – ③ + ④

Formula application:

1. "x" denotes the number of each ear loop.
   "n" denotes the total number of ear loops; "n" is bigger than 4.
2. When the value of "x" is not enough for deduction, then that item does not exist.
   Example x = 3 and insert this into the equation to give ③ + ① + ②
   x = 5 and insert this into the equation to give ⑤ – ① + ② – ③ + ④
3. Use formula "a" for all ear loops except the number 4 by counting backwards.
   Use formula "b" for this particular ear loop.

Type 1 Compound constellation knot.

Type 2 Compound Constellation Knot

This compound knot is made by wrapping a series of ear loops one after the other using the technique of one loop, one wrap.

TYING INSTRUCTIONS
1. Tie the knot following the step-by-step illustration guide below.
2. Use the formula application on page 74 to tie a compound constellation knot with "n" number of outer loops.

HINT
See page 73.

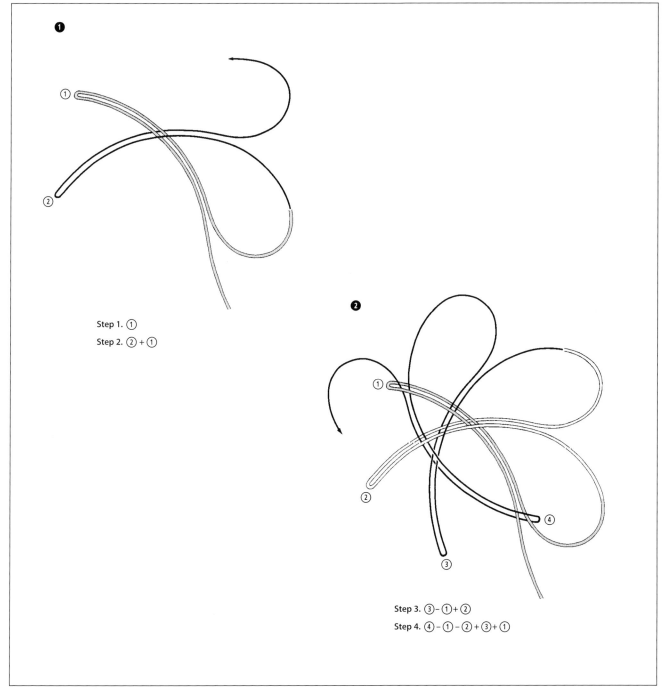

Step 1. ①
Step 2. ② + ①

Step 3. ③ – ① + ②
Step 4. ④ – ① – ② + ③ + ①

❸

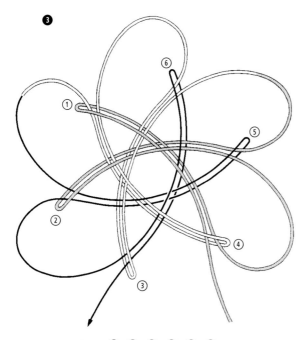

Step 5. ⑤ – ② – ③ + ④ + ① + ②
Step 6. ⑥ – ③ – ④ + ⑤ – ① + ② + ③

❺ Completed knot

❹

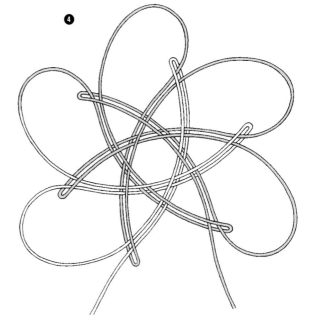

Formula for Type 2 Compound constellation knot with multiple outer loops:
a. (x) – (x–3) – (x–2) + (x–1)
b. (n–2) – (n–2–3) – (n–2–2) + (n–2–1) + ①
   (n–1) – (n–1–3) – (n–1–2) + (n–1–1) + ① + ②
   (n) – (n–3) – (n–2) – (n–1)+ ① – ② + ③

Formula application:
1. "x" denotes the number of each ear loop.
   "n" denotes the total number of ear loops; "n" is bigger than 3.
2. When the value of "x" is not enough for deduction, then that item does not exist.
   Example x = 3 and insert this into the equation to give ③ – ① + ②
            x = 5 and insert this into the equation to give ⑤ – ② – ③ + ④
3. Use formula "a" for all ear loops except the number 3 by counting backwards.
   Use formula "b" for this particular ear loop.

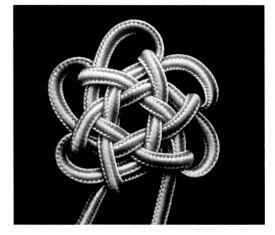

Type 2 Compound constellation knot.

Type 3 Compound Constellation Knot

This compound knot is made by wrapping a series of ear loops twice using the technique of two loops, one wrap.

TYING INSTRUCTIONS
1. Tie the knot following the step-by-step illustration guide below.
2. Use the formula application on page 78 to tie a compound constellation knot with "n" number of outer loops.

HINT
See page 73.

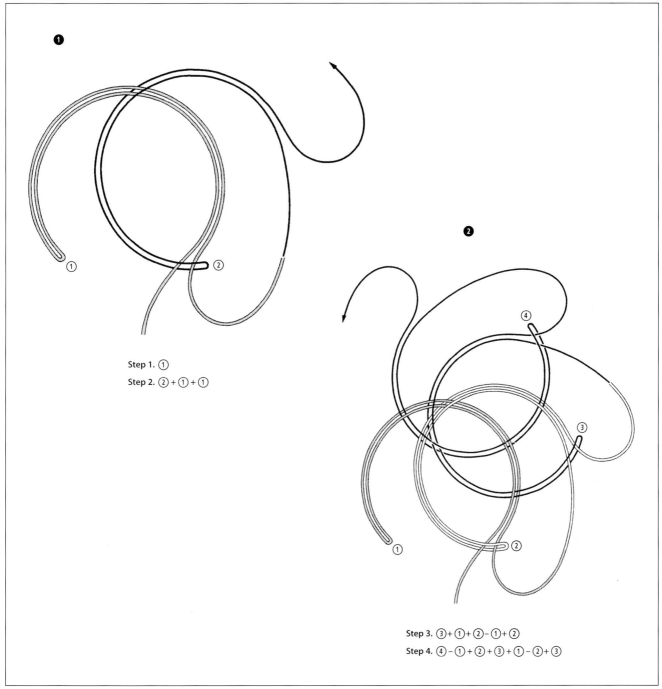

❶

❷

Step 1. ①
Step 2. ② + ① + ①

Step 3. ③ + ① + ② − ① + ②
Step 4. ④ − ① + ② + ③ + ① − ② + ③

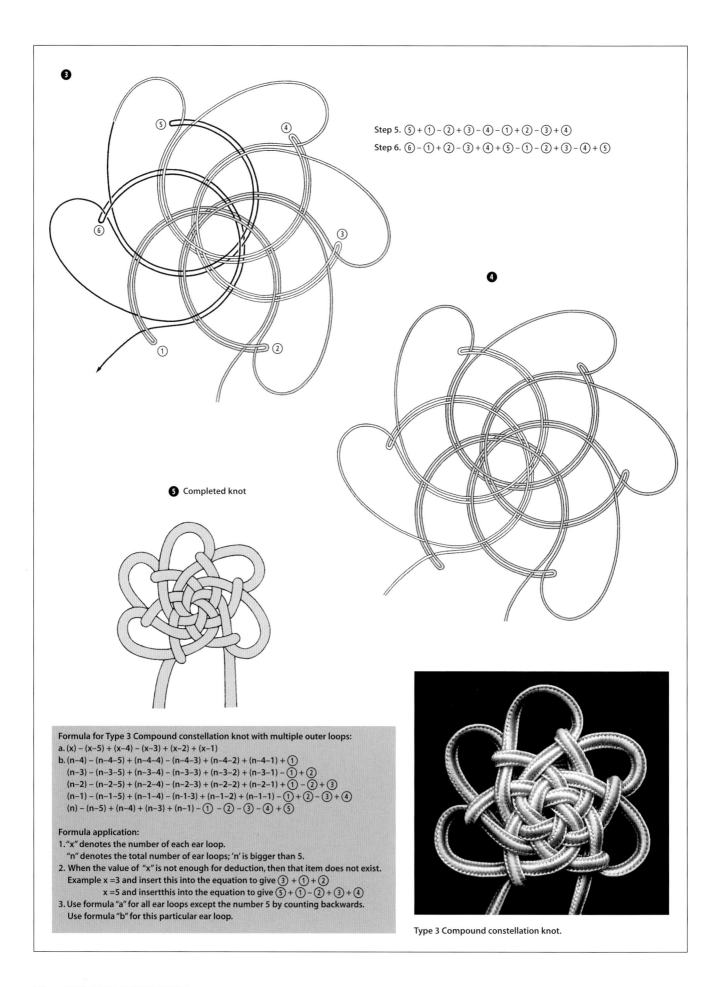

❸

Step 5. ⑤ + ① − ② + ③ − ④ − ① + ② − ③ + ④

Step 6. ⑥ − ① + ② − ③ + ④ + ⑤ − ① − ② + ③ − ④ + ⑤

❹

❺ Completed knot

Formula for Type 3 Compound constellation knot with multiple outer loops:

a. (x) − (x−5) + (x−4) − (x−3) + (x−2) + (x−1)

b. (n−4) − (n−4−5) + (n−4−4) − (n−4−3) + (n−4−2) + (n−4−1) + ①
(n−3) − (n−3−5) + (n−3−4) − (n−3−3) + (n−3−2) + (n−3−1) − ① + ②
(n−2) − (n−2−5) + (n−2−4) − (n−2−3) + (n−2−2) + (n−2−1) + ① − ② + ③
(n−1) − (n−1−5) + (n−1−4) − (n−1−3) + (n−1−2) + (n−1−1) − ① + ② − ③ + ④
(n) − (n−5) + (n−4) + (n−3) + (n−1) − ① − ② − ③ − ④ + ⑤

Formula application:

1. "x" denotes the number of each ear loop.
   "n" denotes the total number of ear loops; 'n' is bigger than 5.

2. When the value of "x" is not enough for deduction, then that item does not exist.
   Example x =3 and insert this into the equation to give ③ + ① + ②
   x =5 and insert this into the equation to give ⑤ + ① − ② + ③ + ④

3. Use formula "a" for all ear loops except the number 5 by counting backwards.
   Use formula "b" for this particular ear loop.

Type 3 Compound constellation knot.

Type 4 Compound Constellation Knot

This compound knot is made by taking an ear loop that wraps every second loop to wrap one more loop in front to produce a knot with five outer loops.

TYING INSTRUCTIONS
1. Tie the knot following the step-by-step illustration guide below.
2. Use the formula application on page 80 to tie a compound constellation knot with "n" number of outer loops.

HINT
See page 73.

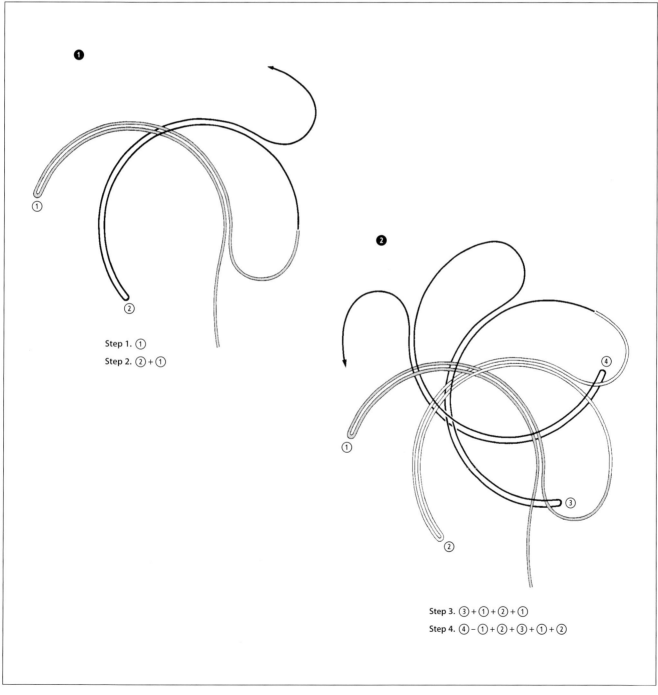

Step 1. ①
Step 2. ② + ①

Step 3. ③ + ① + ② + ①
Step 4. ④ − ① + ② + ③ + ① + ②

❸

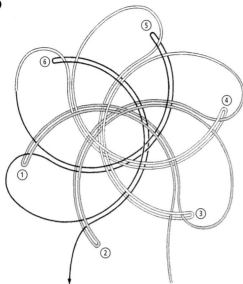

Step 5. ⑤ – ① – ② + ③ + ④ – ① + ② + ③

Step 6. ⑥ – ② – ③ + ④ + ⑤ – ① – ② + ③ + ④

❹

❺ Completed knot

Formula for Type 4 Compound constellation knot with multiple outer loops:
a. (x) – (x–4) – (x–3) + (x–2) + (x – 1)
b. (n–3) – (n–3 –4) – (n–3–3) + (n– 3–2) + (n–3–1) + ①
   (n–2) – (n–2–4) – (n–2–3) + (n–2–2) + (n–2–1) + ① + ②
   (n–1) – (n–1–4) – (n–1–3) + (n–1–2) + (n–1–1) – ① +② +③
   (n) – (n–4) – (n–3) + (n–2) + (n–1) – ① – ② + ③ + ④

Formula application:
1. "x" denotes the number of each ear loop.
  "n" denotes the total number of ear loops; "n" is bigger than 4.
2. When the value of "x" is not enough for deduction, then that item does not exist.
  Example x = 3 and insert this into the equation to give ③+① +②
      x = 5 and insert this into the equation to give ⑤–①–②+③+④
3. Use formula "a" for all ear loops except the number 4 by counting backwards.
  Use formula "b" for this particular ear loop.

Type 4 Compound constellation knot.

Good Luck Knot

This knot is made by wrapping three, four, five, six or more outer loops clockwise or anticlockwise and pulling them firmly to secure them. If careful attention is paid to the tightening process, the knot can also be tied with compound petals – a small circle of loops in between the large outer ones – by pressing loops in the same direction and inserting them into another loop. A great variety of elegant modified good luck knots can thus be obtained by changing the method and number of overlapped and pulled cords. The various types of modified good luck knots are shown below.

Modified Knots

Increasing the Number of Outer Loops

Although the number of outer loops in a good luck knot can be increased infinitely, this leads to a bigger central hole and a looser, less stable knot body. One remedy is to wrap every second or more ear loop instead of the adjacent one. Another is to limit the number of outer loops to four or five, otherwise it can be difficult to control the shape of the finished knot.

Modified Knot Bodies

Changing the Method of Wrapping and Pulling

By knotting the first layer of the good luck knot using the basic wrap one, pull one knotting technique and then knotting the second layer using a different technique – pressing and inserting – it is possible to achieve a variety of modified knots with different knot body structures. Alternatively, the arrangement of the ear loops can be altered in such a way that new square knots are achieved.

Good luck knot with six outer loops (see page 82).

Good luck knot with compound outer loops (see page 84).

Lingzhi knot (see page 85).

Type 1 Good luck knot with small outer loops (see page 86).

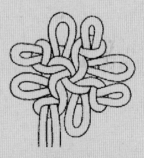

Type 2 Good luck knot with small outer loops (see page 88).

Type 3 Good luck knot with small outer loops (see page 89).

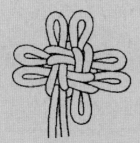

Type 4 Good luck knot with small outer loops (see page 90).

Type 5 Good luck knot with small outer loops (see page 91).

Pan Chang good luck knot (see page 93).

Good Luck Knot with Six Outer Loops

The technique for tying a good luck knot with multiple outer loops is similar to that of the round brocade knot (page 59) except that the knotting process has to be repeated for each ear loop.

TYING INSTRUCTIONS
Step 1. Make (i.e. fold and arrange) double ear loop 1. **Step 2.** Make double ear loop 2 and pull through 1. **Step 3.** Make double ear loop 3 and pull through 1 and 2. **Step 4.** Make double ear loop 4 and pull through 2 and 3. **Step 5.** Make double ear loop 5, pull through 3 and 4 and wrap around 1. **Step 6.** Make double ear loop 6, pull through 4 and 5 and wrap around 1 and 2.

HINT
To prevent a big central hole, wrap every third, fourth or more loop.

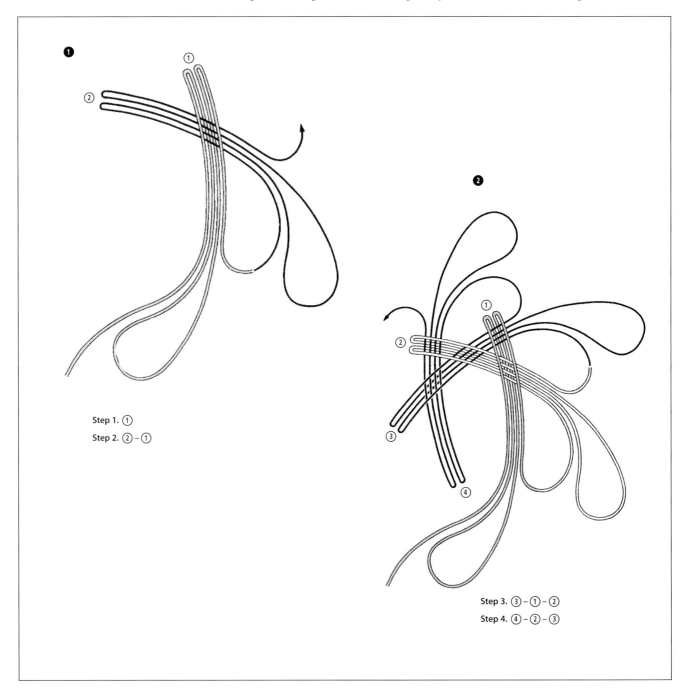

Step 1. ①
Step 2. ② – ①

Step 3. ③ – ① – ②
Step 4. ④ – ② – ③

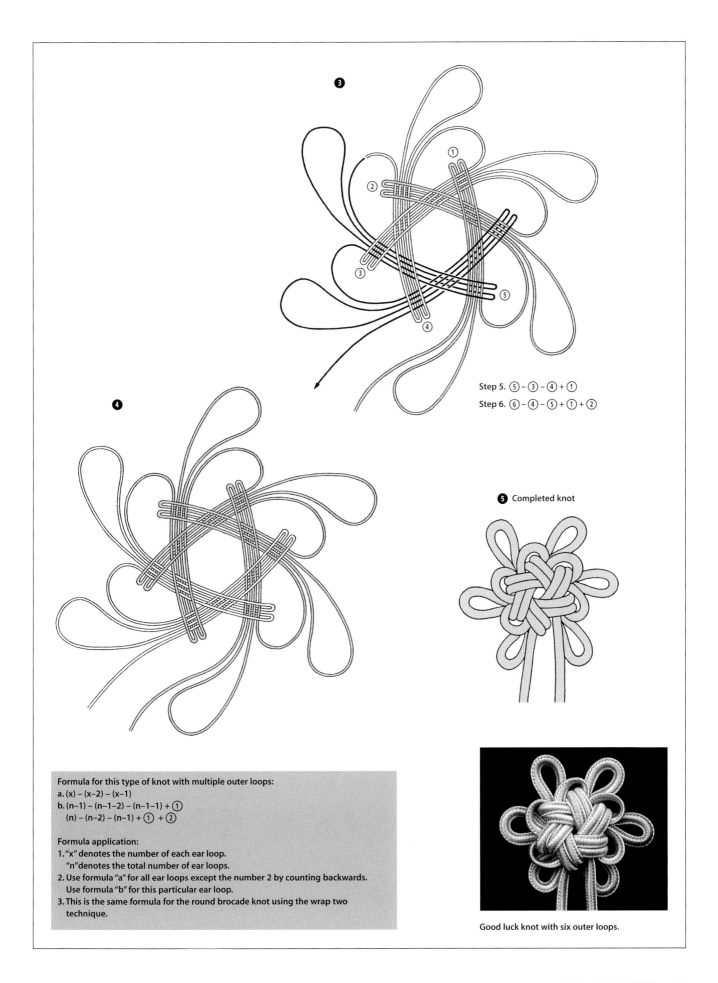

❸

Step 5. ⑤ – ③ – ④ + ①
Step 6. ⑥ – ④ – ⑤ + ① + ②

❹

❺ Completed knot

Formula for this type of knot with multiple outer loops:
a. (x) – (x–2) – (x–1)
b. (n–1) – (n–1–2) – (n–1–1) + ①
   (n) – (n–2) – (n–1) + ① + ②

Formula application:
1. "x" denotes the number of each ear loop.
   "n" denotes the total number of ear loops.
2. Use formula "a" for all ear loops except the number 2 by counting backwards.
   Use formula "b" for this particular ear loop.
3. This is the same formula for the round brocade knot using the wrap two
   technique.

Good luck knot with six outer loops.

Good Luck Knot with Compound Outer Loops

This is an example of a good luck knot with four compound outer loops. Change the knotting technique of the second layer to achieve this compound good luck knot with bigger loops covering smaller ones.

TYING INSTRUCTIONS
Step 1. Tie the first layer using the basic good luck knotting technique. **Step 2.** Tie the back face (i.e. the one without small outer loops) of the second layer in an anti-clockwise direction. Press ear loop 1 on 2 and insert into 3. **Step 3.** Press ear loop 2 on 1 and 3 and insert into 4. **Step 4.** Press ear loop 3 on 2 and 4 and insert into 1. **Step 5.** Press ear loop 4 on 3, pull through 1 and insert into 2. Tighten cords in the direction of the arrows.

HINTS
• Be aware that the shorter outer loops in this knot can shrink easily into the knot body and make it loose.
• To produce a slightly different effect, you can lengthen the outer loops on the inside and shorten those on the outside during the tightening process.

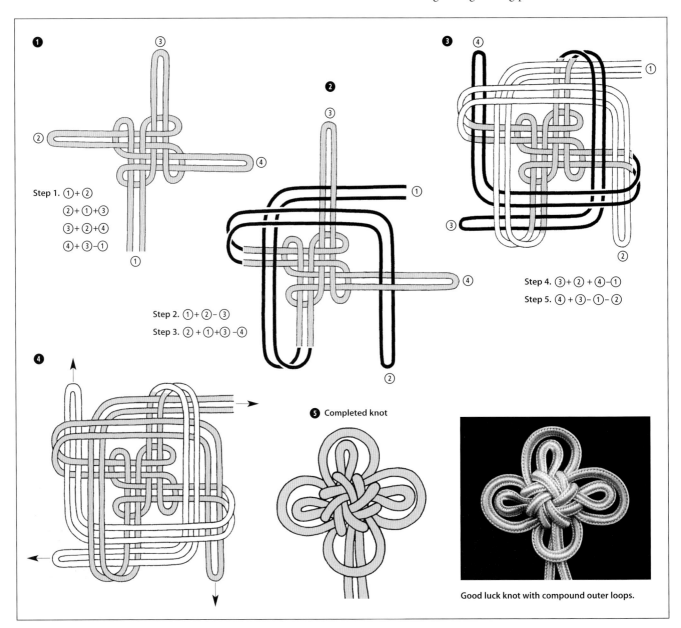

Good luck knot with compound outer loops.

Lingzhi Knot

This is called a *lingzhi* knot because of its close resemblance to the *lingzhi* good luck fungus. It combines the technique of knotting a good luck knot with compound outer loops with that of the cloverleaf knot. The three cloverleaf knots sit nicely on the small outer loops set within the bigger outer loops. They make the knot look more elegant and prevent the smaller outer loops from working loose.

TYING INSTRUCTIONS
Before tying the good luck knot with compound outer loops, tie the cloverleaf knots on the ear loops. Then follow the steps in the knotting technique of the good luck knot with compound outer loops (see page 84).

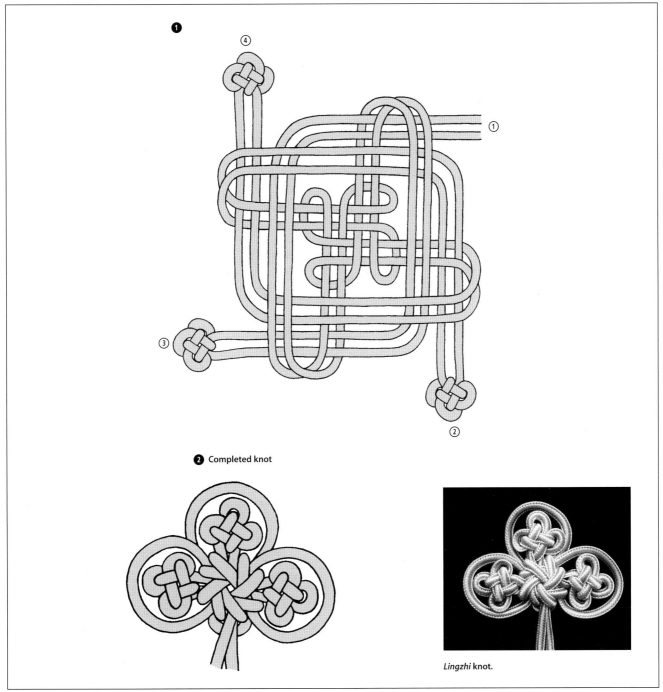

2 Completed knot

Lingzhi knot.

Type 1 Good Luck Knot with Small Outer Loops

Besides adding more ear loops in order to increase the total number of outer loops, it is also possible – after knotting the first layer – to lengthen the small outer loops around the knot body so that they form the second layer of ear loops for overlapping and pressing together. This method not only increases the number of outer loops, but also improves the overall appearance of the knot.

There are five ways of tying modified good luck knots with small outer loops:
1. Lengthening the small outer loops on either the front or back face of the first layer.
2. Lengthening the small ear loops clockwise or anticlockwise.
3. Overlapping and pressing together different numbers of small outer loops to form ear loops for the second layer of the knot body.
4. Doing method 3 clockwise or anticlockwise.
5. Overlapping and pressing together the big and small outer loops to form the second layer of the knot body.

Variations in the tightness of the knot body, the arrangements of big and small outer loops, and the presence or labsence of special lines all produce different results.

For the five types of modified good luck knots taught here, the first layer of each is tied anticlockwise using the basic good luck knotting technique. The second layer is done by lengthening and knotting the small outer loops clockwise.

For Type 1 Good Luck Knot with Small Outer Loops, working clockwise, pull out each small outer loop on the back of the first layer to lengthen it. Systematically press every other loop and insert it into the next loop.

TYING INSTRUCTIONS
Step 1. Tie the first layer using the basic good luck knotting technique, then pull out each small outer loop on the back. **Step 2.** For the second layer, press small outer loop 1 on 2 and insert into 3. **Step 3.** Press small outer loop 2 on 1 and 3 and insert into 4. **Step 4.** Press small outer loop 3 on 2 and 4 and insert into 1. **Step 5.** Press small outer loop 4 on 3, pull through 1 and insert into 2. Tighten the cords in the direction of the arrows.

HINTS
• When lengthening the small outer loops on the first layer, do this anticlockwise on the front and clockwise on the back to prevent the knot body becoming loose.
• When lengthening the small outer loops, anchor the long and short outer loops on a piece of chipboard or a cardboard box with round-head pins to prevent the loops getting messed up and the body misshapen in the second round.

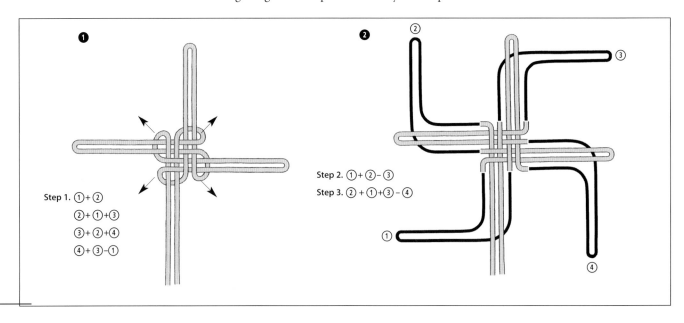

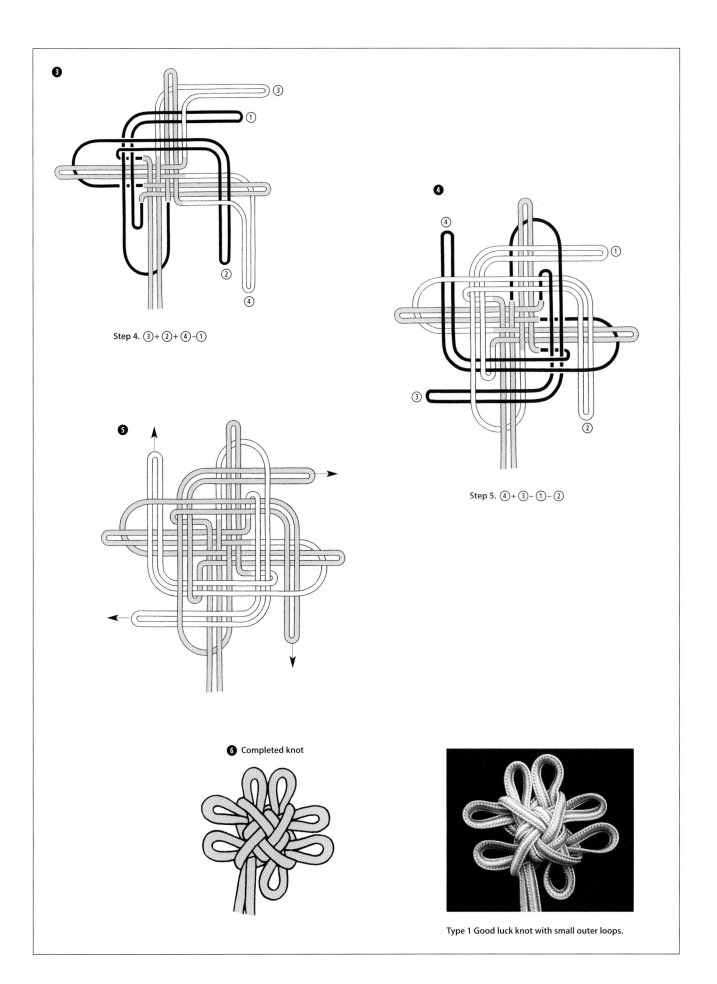

Step 4. ③ + ② + ④ − ①

Step 5. ④ + ③ − ① − ②

6 Completed knot

Type 1 Good luck knot with small outer loops.

Type 2 Good Luck Knot with Small Outer Loops

Lengthen the small outer loops anticlockwise on the back of the first layer, then systematically press down every second small outer loop and insert into the next loop.

TYING INSTRUCTIONS
Step 1. Tie the first layer using the basic good luck knotting technique, then pull out each small outer loop on the back. **Step 2.** Press small outer loop 1 on 2 and insert into 3. **Step 3.** Press small outer loop 2 on 1 and 3 and insert into 4. **Step 4.** Press small outer loop 3 on 2 and 4 and insert into 1. **Step 5.** Press small outer loop 4 on 3, pull through 1 and insert into 2. Tighten cords in the direction of the arrows.

HINTS
See page 86.

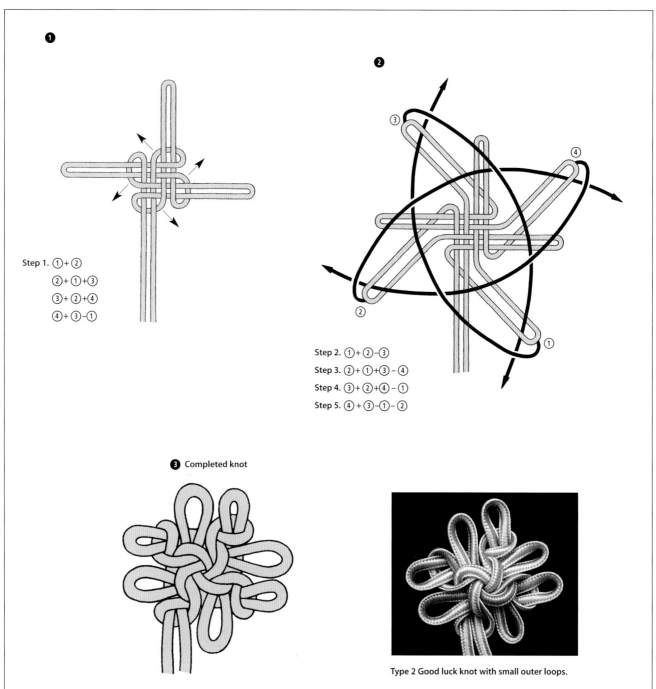

Step 1. ①+②
    ②+①+③
    ③+②+④
    ④+③−①

Step 2. ①+②−③
Step 3. ②+①+③−④
Step 4. ③+②+④−①
Step 5. ④+③−①−②

❸ Completed knot

Type 2 Good luck knot with small outer loops.

Type 3 Good Luck Knot with Small Outer Loops

On the front of the first layer, lengthen the small outer loops clockwise, and systematically press every second loop and insert into the next one.

TYING INSTRUCTIONS
Step 1. Tie the first layer using the basic good luck knotting technique, then pull out each small outer loop on the back. **Step 2.** Press small outer loop 1 on 2 and insert into 3. **Step 3.** Press small outer loop 2 on 1 and 3 and insert into 4. **Step 4.** Press small outer loop 3 on 2 and 4 and insert into 1. **Step 5.** Press small outer loop 4 on 3, pull through 1 and insert into 2. Tighten cords in the direction of the arrows.

HINTS
See page 86.

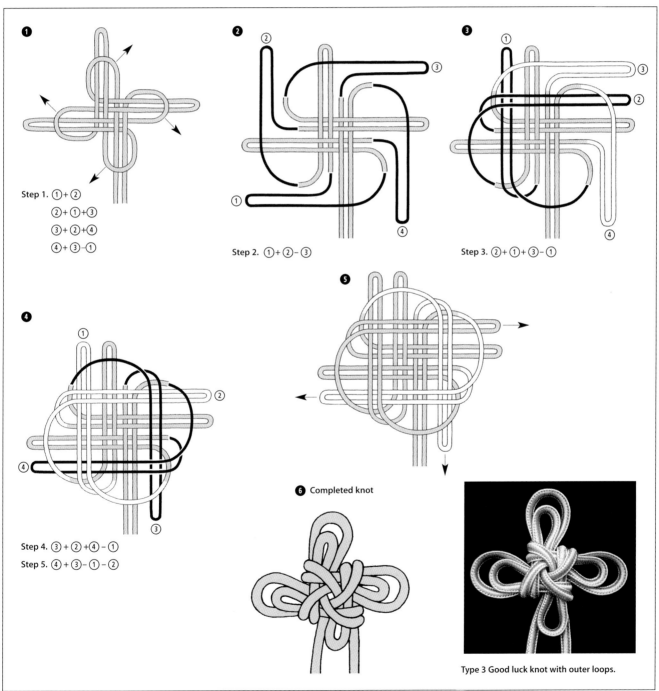

❶

Step 1. ①+②
②+①+③
③+②+④
④+③-①

❷

Step 2. ①+②-③

❸

Step 3. ②+①+③-①

❹

Step 4. ③+②+④-①
Step 5. ④+③-①-②

❺

❻ Completed knot

Type 3 Good luck knot with outer loops.

Type 4 Good Luck Knot with Small Outer Loops

Lengthen the small outer loops clockwise on the back of the first layer, and press down every second loop.

TYING INSTRUCTIONS

Step 1. Tie the first layer using the basic good luck knotting technique, then pull out each small outer loop on the back. **Step 2.** Press small outer loop 1 on 2 and insert into 3. **Step 3.** Press small outer loop 2 on 1 and 3 and insert into 4. **Step 4.** Press small outer loop 3 on 2 and 4 and insert into 1. **Step 5.** Press small outer loop 4 on 3, pull through 1 and insert into 2. Tighten cords in the direction of the arrows.

HINTS

See page 86.

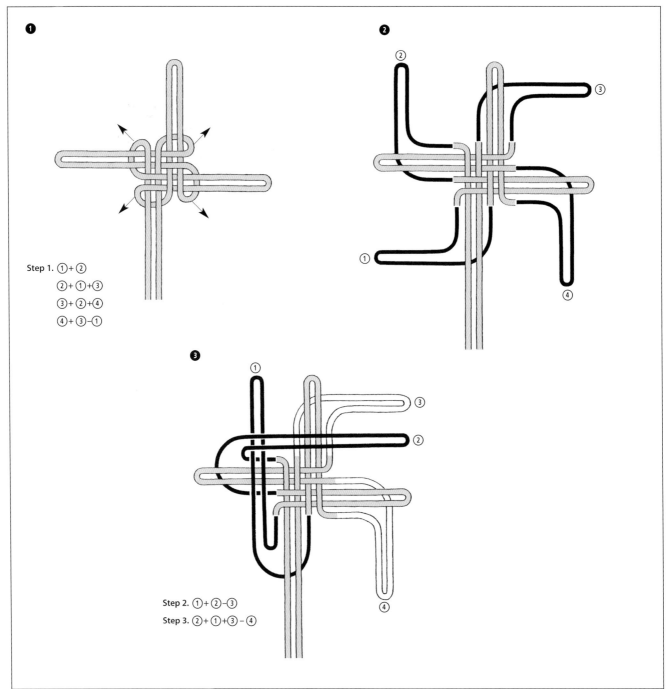

Step 1. ①+②
　　　　②+①+③
　　　　③+②+④
　　　　④+③−①

Step 2. ①+②−③
Step 3. ②+①+③−④

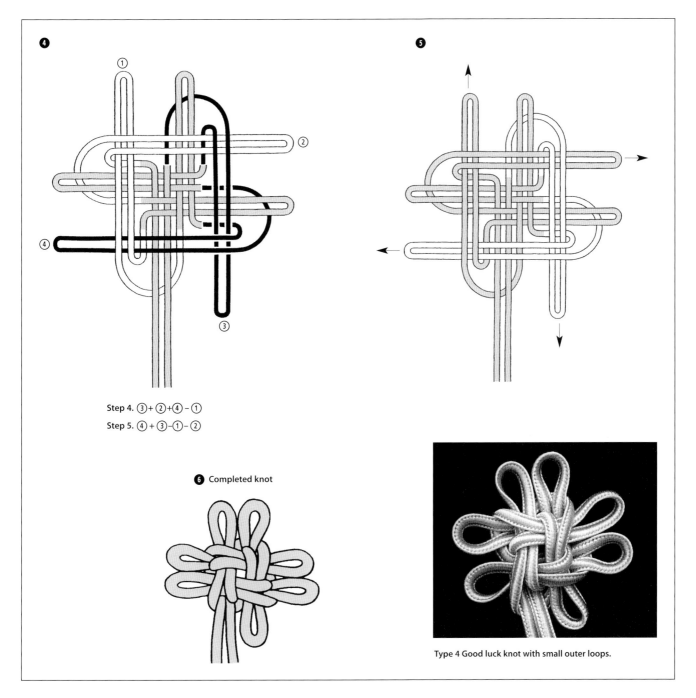

Step 4. ③ + ② + ④ − ①
Step 5. ④ + ③ − ① − ②

6 Completed knot

Type 4 Good luck knot with small outer loops.

Type 5 Good Luck Knot with Small Outer Loops

Lengthen the small outer loops clockwise on the front of the first layer, and press every second loop.

TYING INSTRUCTIONS
Step 1. Tie the first layer using the basic good luck knotting technique, then pull out each small outer loop on the back. **Step 2.** Press small outer loop 1 on 2 and insert into 3. **Step 3.** Press small outer loop 2 on 1 and 3 and insert into 4. **Step 4.** Press small outer loop 3 on 2 and 4 and insert into 1. **Step 5.** Press small outer loop 4 on 3, pull through 1 and insert into 2. Tighten cords in the direction of the arrows.

HINTS
See page 86.

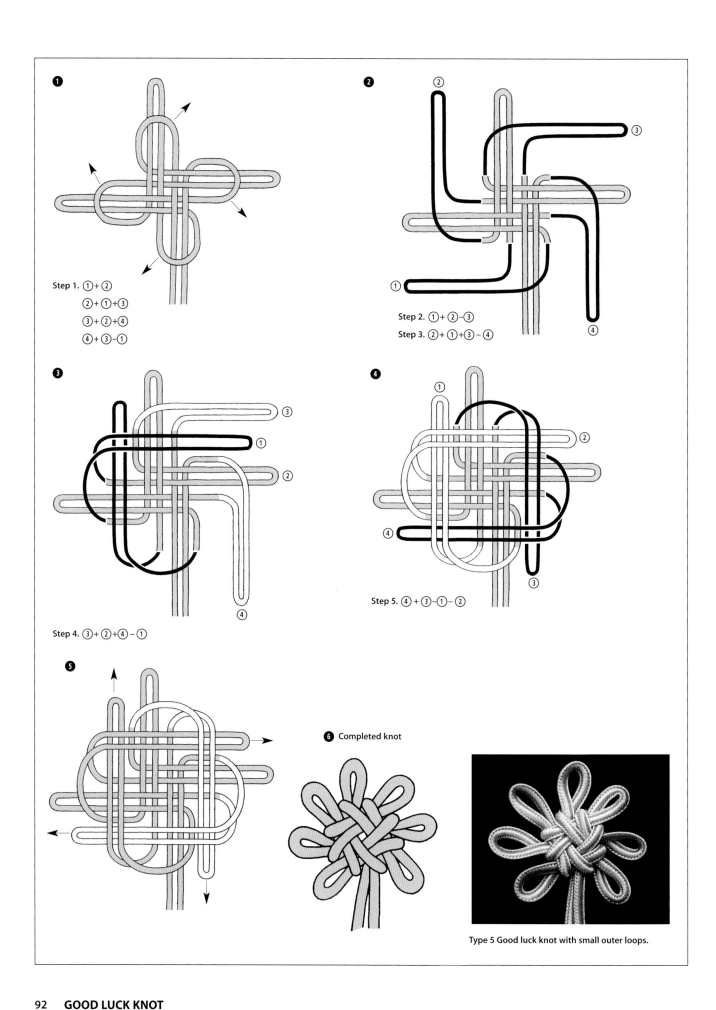

❶

Step 1. ①+②
②+①+③
③+②+④
④+③−①

❷

Step 2. ①+②−③
Step 3. ②+①+③−④

❸

Step 4. ③+②+④−①

❹

Step 5. ④+③−①−②

❺

❻ Completed knot

Type 5 Good luck knot with small outer loops.

Pan Chang Good Luck Knot

The *pan chang* good luck knot is a square good luck knot. The knotting technique for the ear loops on all four sides is the same as for the *pan chang* knot, i.e. the wrap and pull technique is used. The rest of the knot uses the good luck knotting technique, i.e. the press and insert technique. The size of the *pan chang* good luck knot can be controlled by varying the number of ear loops. The knot can also be made with compound/overlapped outer loops by changing the knotting sequence of the ear loops. This knot is usually tied with eight outer loops.

TYING INSTRUCTIONS
1. Use the *pan chang* knotting technique to line up the ear loops on all four sides. If you are knotting clockwise with a single cord end, you must arrange the loops on the first three sides using the pull technique, i.e. pulled underneath the ear loop.
2. Use the press one, pull one technique on the last side. If you knot with two cord ends, then use the *pan chang* style, i.e. use the press technique on one side, the pull technique on the other, and the press one, pull one technique on the last side. Repeat the process on the ear loops.

HINT
When tying the first layer, make sure that the linked cords between the ear loops are wrapped around the loop coming from the opposite side.

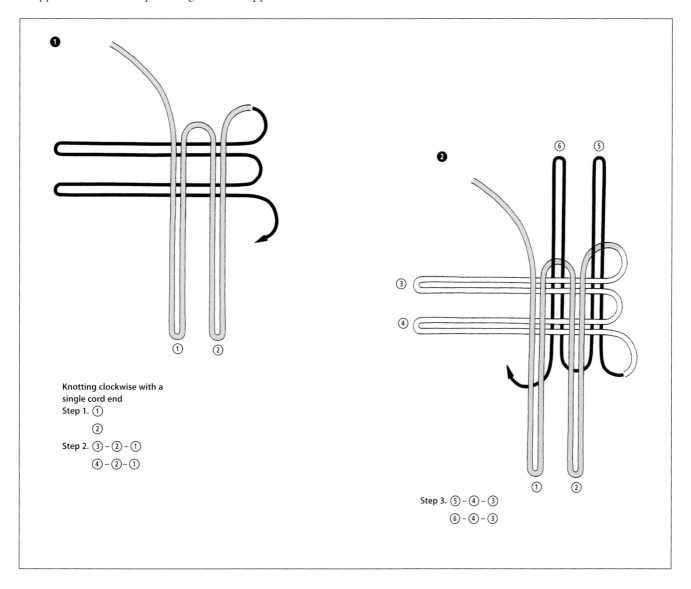

Knotting clockwise with a single cord end
Step 1. ①
        ②
Step 2. ③ – ② – ①
        ④ – ② – ①

Step 3. ⑤ – ④ – ③
        ⑥ – ④ – ③

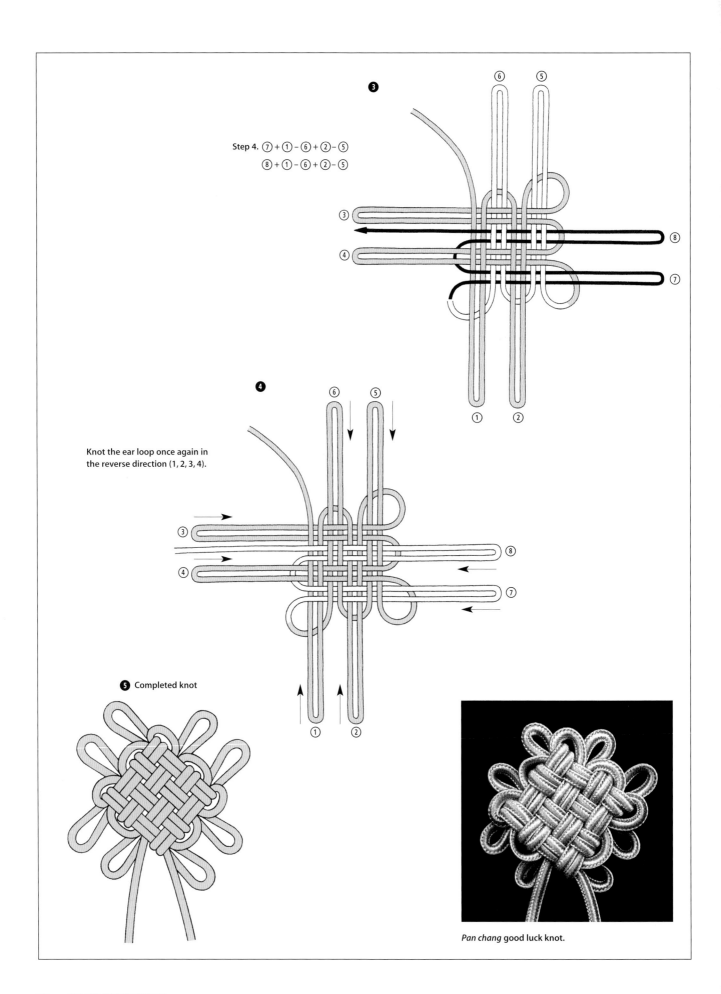

③

Step 4. ⑦ + ① – ⑥ + ② – ⑤
⑧ + ① – ⑥ + ② – ⑤

④

Knot the ear loop once again in the reverse direction (1, 2, 3, 4).

⑤ Completed knot

Pan chang good luck knot.

Buddha Knot

The Buddha knot is a primitive religious symbol or ornament in the shape of a Greek cross, usually with the ends of the arms bent at right angles in either a clockwise or anticlockwise direction. In Chinese Buddhist symbolism, the arms of the symbol are bent anticlockwise. The Buddha knot represents the Buddha's heart and has come to stand for the accumulation of good fortune and complete virtue, a symbol of Buddhahood and of the Buddha himself.

Modified Knots

The Buddha knot is made by hooking up two flat knots and pulling them tightly outwards from the center. A simple knot is tied and then another, with the second knot hooking through the loop of the first. The cord between the simple knots becomes the top loop as each of the linked loops is drawn through the center of its opposite knot. When the knot is pulled tight, first horizontally and then vertically, the cross-like shape will appear naturally. Because it is a very simple knot, even when the left and right flat knots are interchanged and/or the loops are pulled to different lengths, there is very little difference in the appearance of the knot.

Modified Knot Bodies

The weave direction and tightening method of the flat knot can produce different knots, such as the strap knot and the loopless Buddha knot shown below, although these do not vary a great deal from the basic Buddha knot.

Strap knot (see page 96).

Loopless Buddha knot (see page 97).

Strap Knot

This is done by hooking up two flat knots of the same weave, then tightening them using the Buddha knot method. A loose knot is formed in this way. The Japanese like to use the strap knot for decoration.

TYING INSTRUCTIONS
Step 1. Tie a simple knot, then tie another with the cord hooking through the loop of the first. **Steps 2, 3.** Pull the knot tight, first horizontally, then vertically.

HINT
This is not a very stable knot and has to be pulled very tight to keep its shape, especially if synthetic cord is used. Once the desired shape is set, you might want to stitch the body of the knot together.

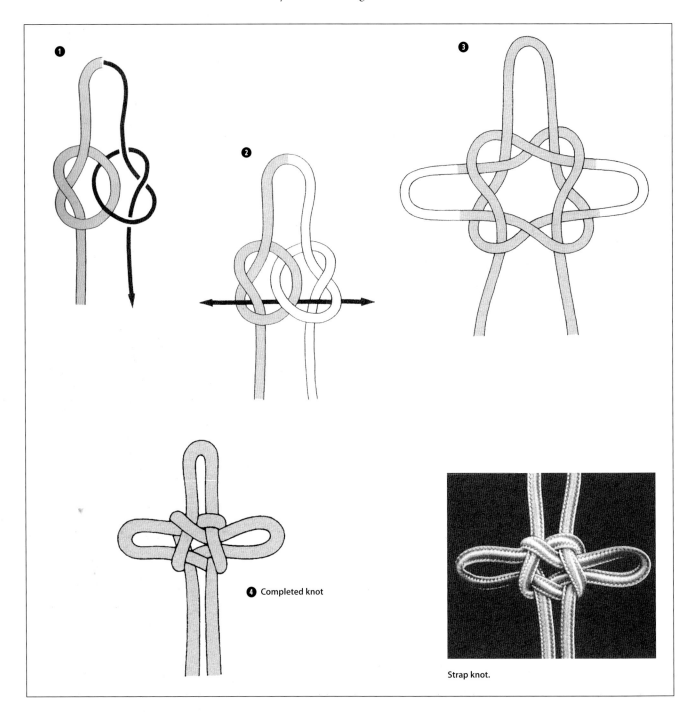

❹ Completed knot

Strap knot.

Loopless Buddha Knot

This is made by using the Buddha knot technique (page 96) followed by tightening outwards vertically only.

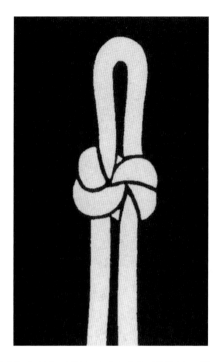

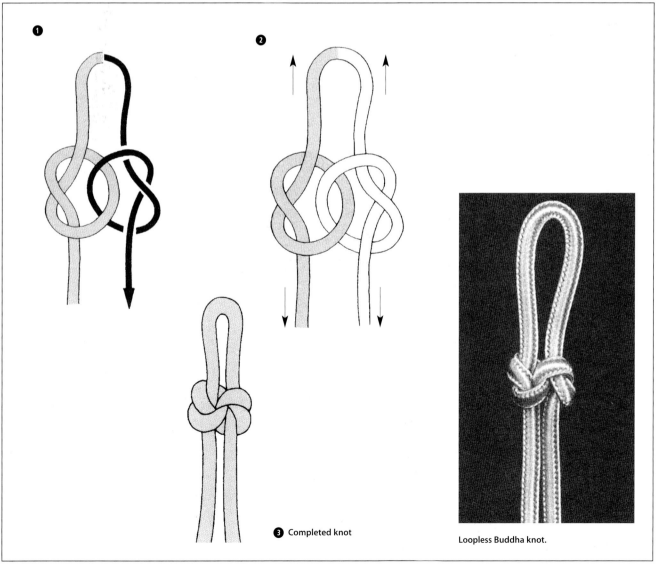

1

2

3 Completed knot

Loopless Buddha knot.

Double Connection Knot

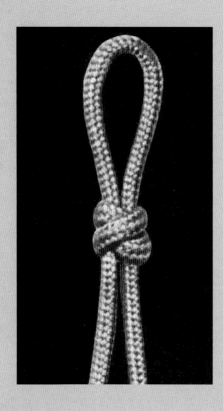

The double connection knot is exactly what its name suggests – two knots tied into one another and then pulled together. Half of one flat knot forms half of the other. The result is a knot with a tight body but no outer loops. Different double connection knots can be achieved by varying the number of flat knots that are included and the method of hooking them up. The different types of double connection knots are shown below.

Modified Knots

The knotting technique of the double connection knot involves hooking up two flat knots followed by vertical tightening. One cord end is used to tie a flat knot around the other cord end. Then the other cord end is used to tie a flat knot around the first cord end, linking through the loop of the first flat knot. The "x" pattern will appear naturally if the cord is pulled from both top and bottom of the knot with equal force. Generally, the double connection knot is a very simple knot without a great deal of variation possible in its structure.

Modified Knot Bodies

The number of flat knots and the method of hooking them up can be varried to produce a horizontal double connection knot, a single loop double connection knot and a long double connection knot.

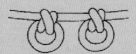

Single loop double connection knot (see page 100).

Horizontal double connection knot (see page 99).

Long double connection knot (see page 101).

Horizontal Double Connection Knot

This modified double connection knot is made by tying two flat knots and tightening them horizontally. The unique characteristic of the knot is that the two cord ends emerge from the left and right sides of the knot body. Because a single knot by itself has little impact, a series of knots is normally tied together to form a "tassel." This is ideal for decorating an object as the long series of knots form the tassel head and the two cord ends the tassel tail.

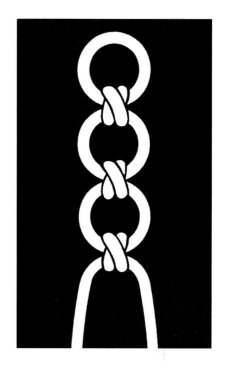

TYING INSTRUCTIONS
Step 1. Press the right cord end over the left cord section and tie an ear loop around it anticlockwise. Pull the right cord end through itself and tie a flat knot. **Step 2.** Use the left cord end to tie an ear loop clockwise around the flat knot tied with the right cord end. Then pull the left cord end through itself and tie a flat knot. **Step 3.** Pull the left cord end and left cord section together towards the right. At the same time, pull the right cord end and right cord section together towards the right.

HINT
Before tightening any double connection knot, adjust the flat knots with your fingers in the way you desire and then only tighten the knot.

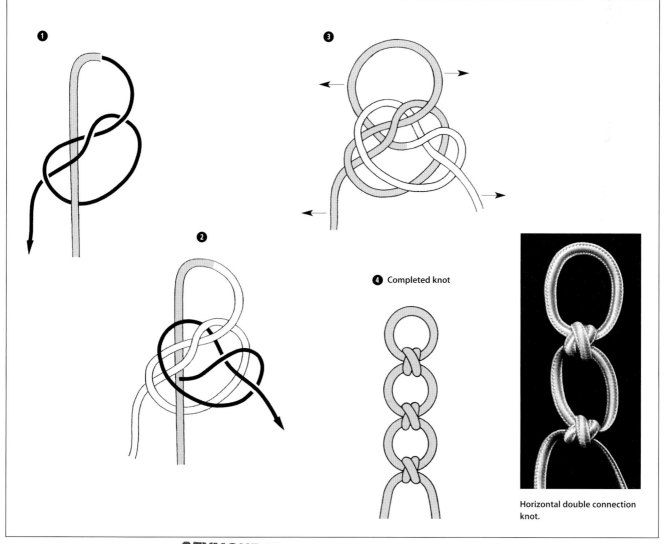

❹ Completed knot

Horizontal double connection knot.

Single Loop Double Connection Knot

The single loop double connection knot is made by tying a horizontal double connection knot with a single cord end. A series of the knots produces a belt-like arrangement. The single loops resemble hollow circles in which beads can be inserted to make a pendant or bracelet or the trim for a blouse or dress.

TYING INSTRUCTIONS
Tie the knot following the step-by-step illustration guide below.

HINT
Keep in mind the desired space between each single loop double connection knot and the knot tied before it.

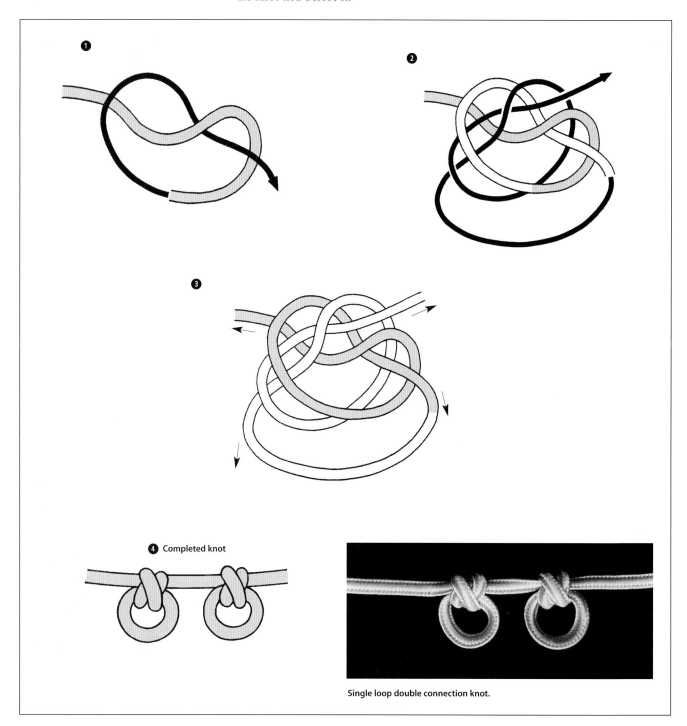

❶

❷

❸

❹ Completed knot

Single loop double connection knot.

Long Double Connection Knot

This modified knot differs slightly from the basic double connection knot in that more flat knots are tied into each other along the central axis.

TYING INSTRUCTIONS
Step 1. Tie each cord end into a flat knot and hook them up. Then pull the right cord end downwards through the left cord section and tie an ear loop clockwise around it. Continue upwards, passing the cord over itself (i.e. the right cord section) and tying a flat knot. **Step 2.** Starting from the bottom right, weave the left cord end all the way around the figure of 8 formed by the right cord, then pull the left cord end downwards through both holes in the figure 8. **Step 3.** Pull the cord loop and both cord ends vertically outwards to tighten the knot.

HINT
Keep in mind the desired size of the top loop or the space between the long double connection knot and the next one to be tied, as the case may be. These will become much larger than they seem to be before tightening.

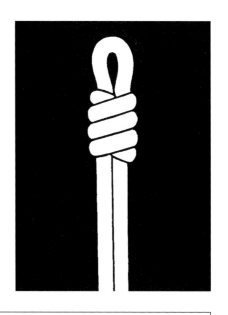

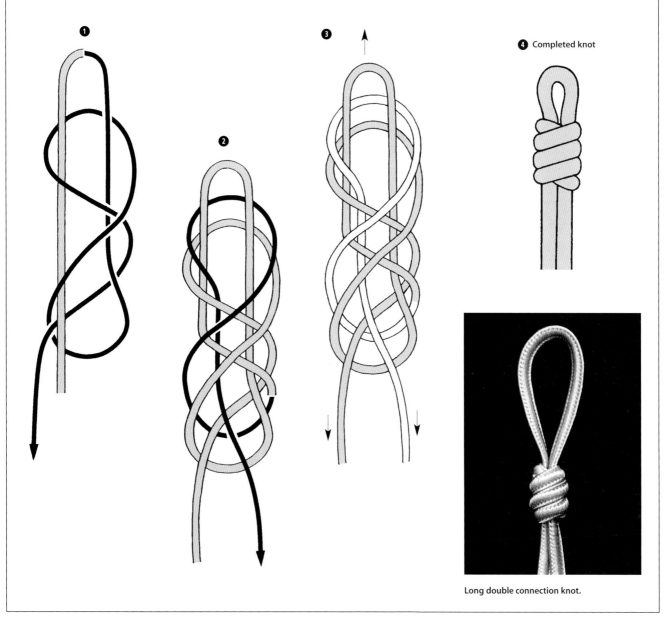

Long double connection knot.

Plafond Knot

The plafond knot, with its spiral-like center and rectangular border, was inspired by the decorations found on the dome-like central sections of ceilings in Chinese temples and palaces. The ceilings, which are divided into nine rectangular sections, three across and three deep, each have a domed apex composed of a circular design filled with auspicious motifs surrounded by a complementary motif which radiates out to the rectangular border. This effect is echoed in the plafond knot, which is made by hooking up and tightening a number of flat knots.

Modified Knots

The knotting technique of the basic plafond knot involves tying horseshoe-shaped flat knots around a central axis, followed by vertical and horizontal tightening. One cord end is used to make a double horseshoe shape around the original loop, tying a flat knot into itself before coming down to the bottom. The second cord end then passes through the bottom of this flat knot, around through the ends of the first horseshoe, under the original loop and through the top of the first flat knot to make a horseshoe of its own. On its way down, it weaves through the central knot to make a symmetrical pattern.

Modified Knot Bodies

As the body of the plafond knot is simple and loopless, it does not lend itself to much modification. However, the basic plafond knot can be varied by altering the number and the direction of the flat knots to produce the long plafond knot, and by changing the knotting technique to produce the horizontal plafond knot.

Long plafond knot (see page 103).

Horizontal plafond knot (see page 105).

Long Plafond Knot

This modified plafond knot is made by altering the number and the direction of the flat knots employed in the basic plafond knot.

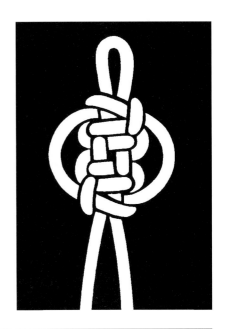

TYING INSTRUCTIONS
1. Tie the flat knots following the step-by-step illustration guide below, then tighten them vertically and horizontally. The easiest method is to tie six flat knots (1, 2, 3, 4, 5 and 6) one after the other using both cord ends, with the weave of knots 3 and 4 or 3 and 5 different from that of the other four.
2. Before tightening, flip flat knots 6, 5 and 4 upwards to alter the arrangement of the flat knots, from top to bottom, into 4, 5, 6, 1, 2 and 3.

HINT
To pull the cord ends through the flat knots, insert your left thumb into the knot and pull the cord ends from the top of the front and back body of the knot.

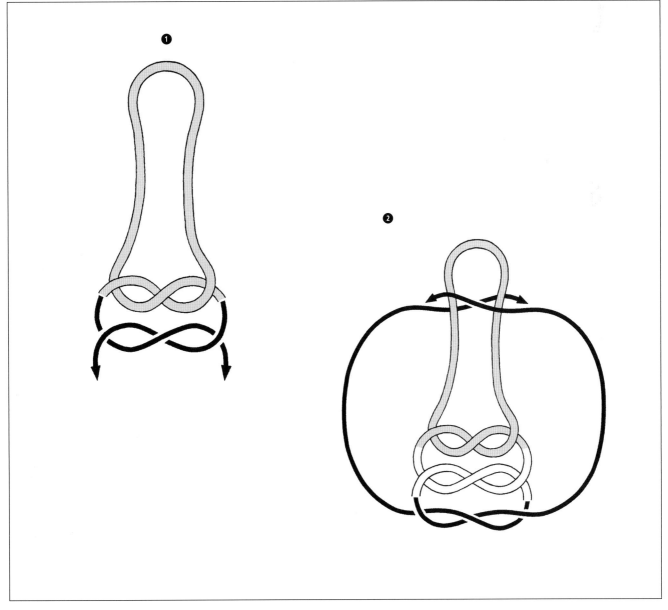

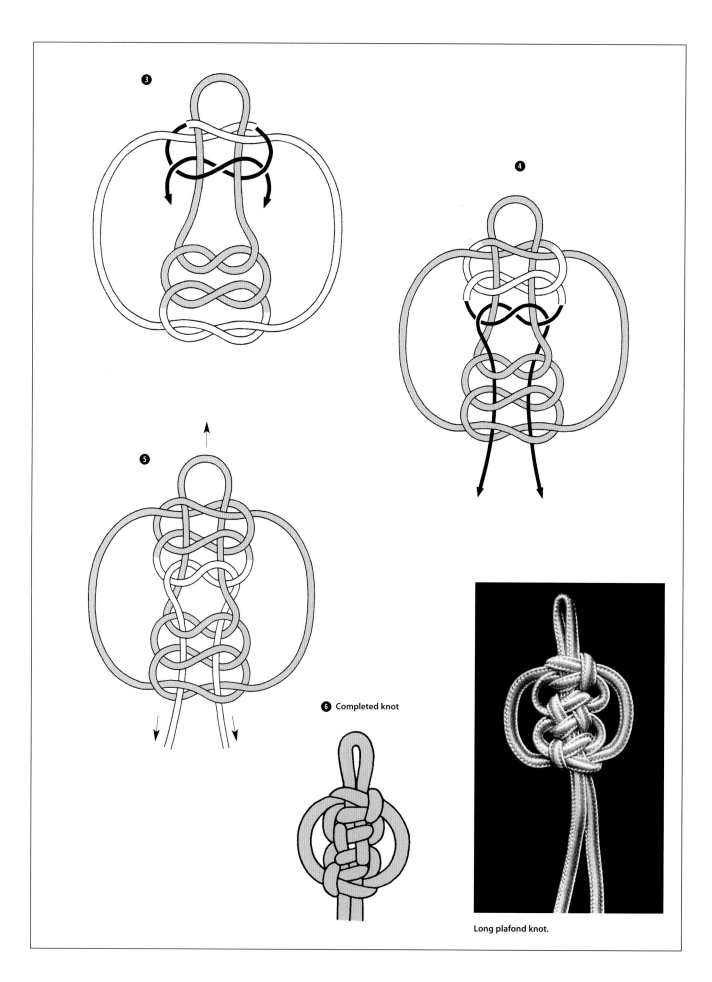

❻ Completed knot

Long plafond knot.

Horizontal Plafond Knot

This consists of two flat knots tied horizontally into swastika knots, with the knot body tightened vertically.

TYING INSTRUCTIONS

Steps 1, 2. Hook up two opposing flat knots, pulling the loops and cord ends tightly outwards from the center. **Step 3.** Pull the top outer loop of the knot downwards towards the cord ends, making sure that the left side of the top loop passes over the left outer loop and the right side of the top loop passes under the right outer loop. **Step 4.** Tie each cord end into a flat knot with the pulled down cord section. Pass the left cord end over the pulled down top loop, behind the left outer loop and up through the left part of the top loop. Pass the right cord end under the pulled down top loop, in front of the right outer loop and up through the right part of the top loop. In this way, both flat knots will separately wrap around the left and right outer loops. **Step 5.** Tighten the knot outwards vertically.

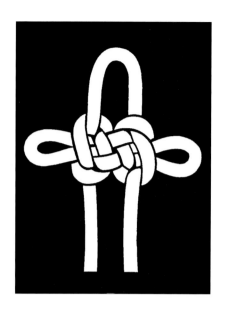

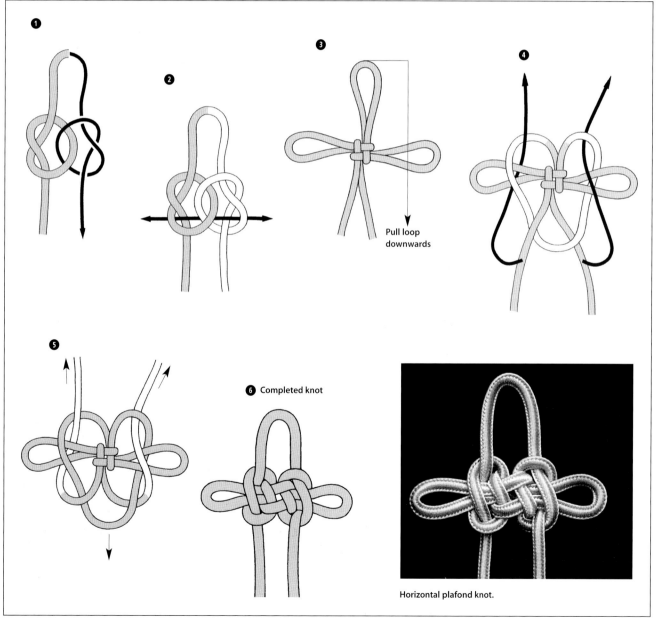

3 Pull loop downwards

6 Completed knot

Horizontal plafond knot.

Double Coin Knot

The double coin knot represents two antique Chinese coins overlapping one another, which connotes both prosperity and longevity. It is a flat knot without outer loops, made by overlapping and stringing a series of ear loops together. Some of the different types of modified double coin knots are shown below. Others are taught in the author's *Chinese Knotting: Creative Designs That Are Easy and Fun!* and *Fun with Chinese Knotting: Making Your Own Fashion Accessories and Accents*.

Modified Knots

The priciple of press one, pull one can be used to extend the length of the basic double coin knot to produce the broad double coin or long double coin knot.

Ten accord knot (see page 86, *Chinese Knotting*).

Broad double coin knot (see page 107).

Long double coin knot (see page 108).

Compound double coin knot (see page 109).

Modified Knot Bodies

A compound double coin knot can be made using the press one, pull one technique of the double coin knot, but with four cord ends. If a single cord end is used, a ring-like pattern – called the round compound double coin knot – is formed.

Below are two formulae for making "n" numbers of odd number round double coin knots (see page 110) and even number round double coin knots (see page 111).

Five happiness knot (see page 86, *Fun with Chinese Knotting*).

Six unity knot (see page 105, *Fun with Chinese Knotting*).

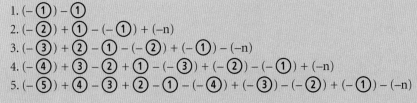

Odd number round compound double coin knot (see page 110).

Even number round compound double coin knot (see page 111).

Odd Number Round Compound Double Coin Knot

Formula 1: Make an odd number of double coin knots into a ring. Link the knots using a single cord end.

1. $(-①) - ①$
2. $(-②) + ① - (-①) + (-n)$
3. $(-③) + ② - ① - (-②) + (-①) - (-n)$
4. $(-④) + ③ - ② + ① - (-③) + (-②) - (-①) + (-n)$
5. $(-⑤) + ④ - ③ + ② - ① - (-④) + (-③) - (-②) + (-①) - (-n)$

Even Number Round Compound Double Coin Knot

Formula 2: Make an even number of double coin knots into a ring. Link the knots using a single cord end.

1. $(-①) + ①$
2. $(-②) + ① + (-①) - (-n)$
3. $(-③) + ② - ① + (-②) - (-①) + (-n)$
4. $(-④) + ③ - ② + ① + (-③) - (-②) + (-①) - (-n)$
5. $(-⑤) + ④ - ③ + ② - ① + (-④) - (-③) + (-②) - (-①) + (-n)$
6. $(-⑥) + ⑤ - ④ + ③ - ② + ① + (-⑤) - (-④) + (-③) - (-②)$
   $+ (-①) - (-n)$

Broad Double Coin Knot

TYING INSTRUCTIONS

1. The right cord end should follow the path shown in the step-by-step illustration guide below. Use the press technique whenever it comes across a path that it has taken before, i.e. the cord should press over the cord sections that have been laid down.

2. The left cord end should also follow the path in the illustration guide. Use the pull technique whenever it meets the right cord in a north easterly-south westerly direction, and the press technique when it meets the right cord in a north westerly–south easterly direction. Whenever it meets its own cord sections, use the pull technique.

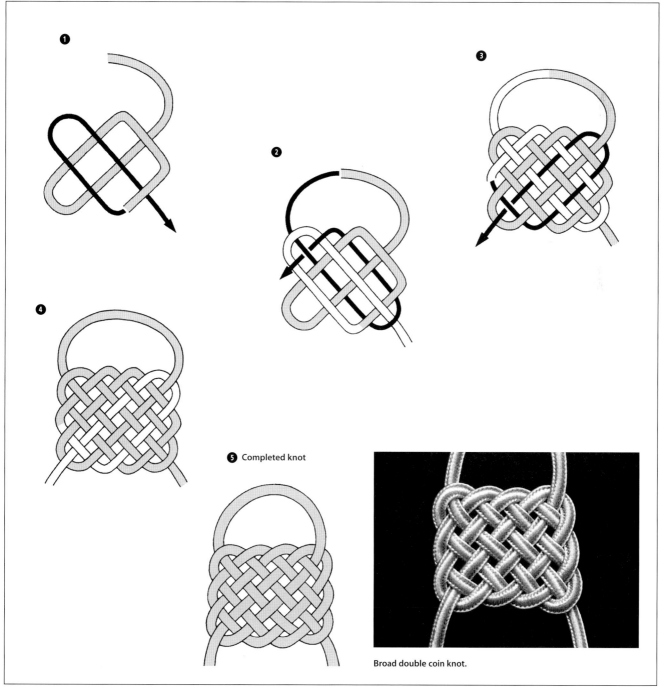

❺ Completed knot

Broad double coin knot.

Long Double Coin Knot

TYING INSTRUCTIONS

1. The two cord ends progress by intertwining around each other to form numerous figures of 8 to the required length. Make sure the cord going from right to left always presses over the other one.

2. Turn back the right cord and snake its way back clockwise according to the press two, pull two technique through every circle until the starting point. Then turn it back again and snake its way back according to the press one, pull one technique until the knot is completed.

HINTS

• When the circle in Step 1 of the illustration guide is an odd number, the cord end in Step 3 must turn back in a clockwise manner and progress according to the press one, pull one technique.

• When the circle in Step 1 of the illustration guide is an even number, the cord end in Step 3 must turn back in an anticlockwise manner and progress according to the press one, pull one technique.

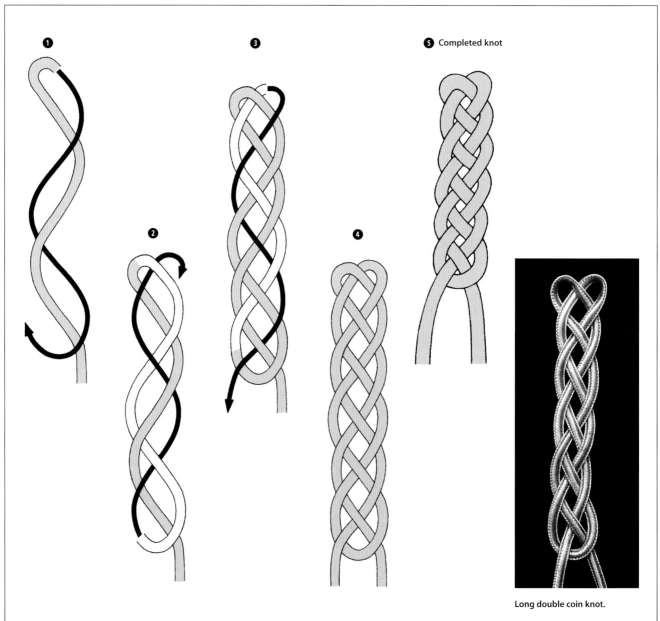

Long double coin knot.

Compound Double Coin Knot

TYING INSTRUCTIONS

1. Knot four cord ends into numerous peach-shaped knots. Since the knot body is flat, all you have to do is to tie and arrange the cords as shown in the illustration guide below.

2. During the tightening process, make sure you tighten more of the horizontal figures of 8 to ensure standardized "peach" formations and hence a more elegant knot.

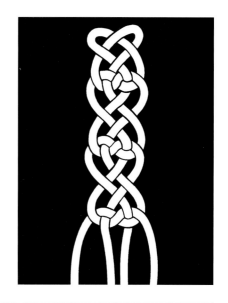

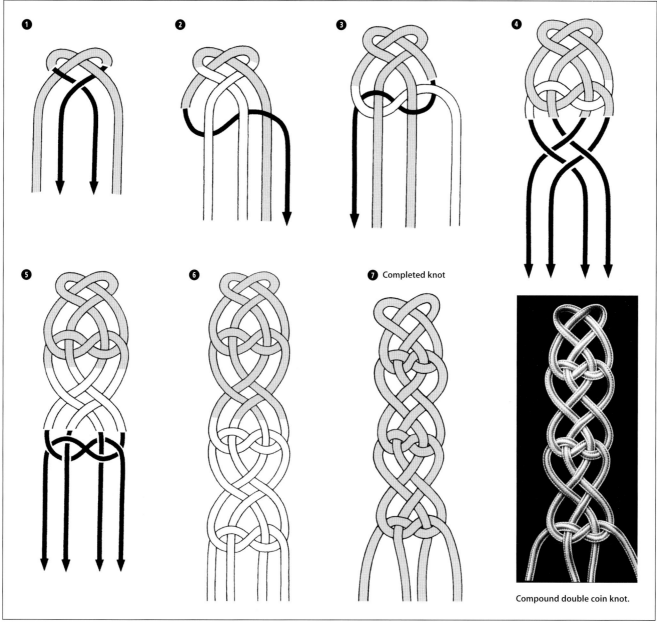

Compound double coin knot.

Odd Number Round Compound Double Coin Knot

A round compound double coin knot is formed when a cord is tied into a circle of double coin knots, with the linked cord in between two knots tied into a new knot body. You can also omit the double coin knots and tie only the new knot body in the center. If you want to tie an "n" number of odd number round compound double coin knots, follow the instructions on page 106.

TYING INSTRUCTIONS
Tie the knot following the illustration guide below. For the arrangement of the central linked cords, see the formula mentioned below.

HINTS
• The right half of an ear loop is designated (+) and the left half (−).
• After completing ear loop 1, turn the cord end clockwise to the left and tie ear loop 2, 3, 4 accordingly until the ear loop (even number) just before the required ear loop (odd number) has been completed.
• Take note of the continuous pull through (−) process in 3, 5, 7 odd number items.

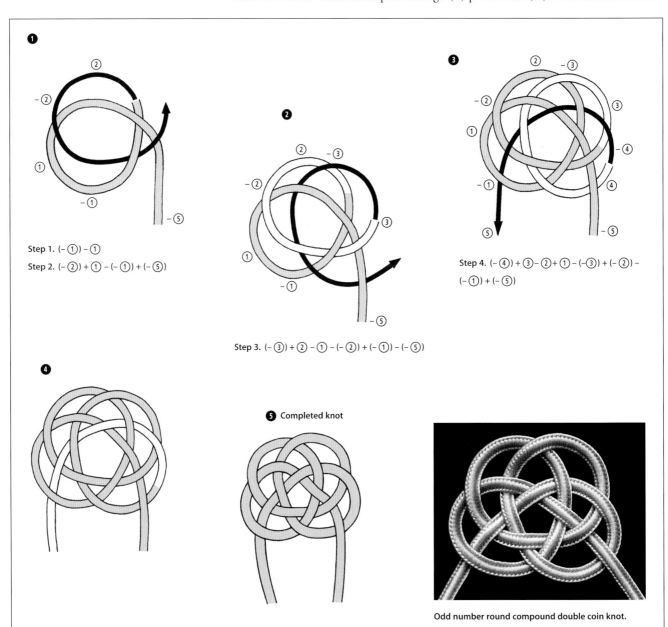

❶
Step 1. (− ①) − ①
Step 2. (− ②) + ① − (− ①) + (− ⑤)

❷
Step 3. (− ③) + ② − ① − (− ②) + (− ①) − (− ⑤)

❸
Step 4. (− ④) + ③ − ② + ① − (−③) + (− ②) − (− ①) + (− ⑤)

❹

❺ Completed knot

Odd number round compound double coin knot.

Even Number Round Compound Double Coin Knot

TYING INSTRUCTIONS

Tie the knot following the illustration guide below. For the arrangement of the central linked cords, see the formula below. If you want to tie an "n" number of even number round compound double coin knots, follow the instructions on page 106.

HINTS
• The right half of the ear loop is designated (+) and the left half (−).
• After completing ear loop 1, turn the cord end anticlockwise to the left and tie ear loop 2, 3, 4 accordingly until the ear loop (odd number) just in front of the required ear loop (even number) has been completed.
• Take note of the continuous press over (+) process of 2, 4, 6 even number items.

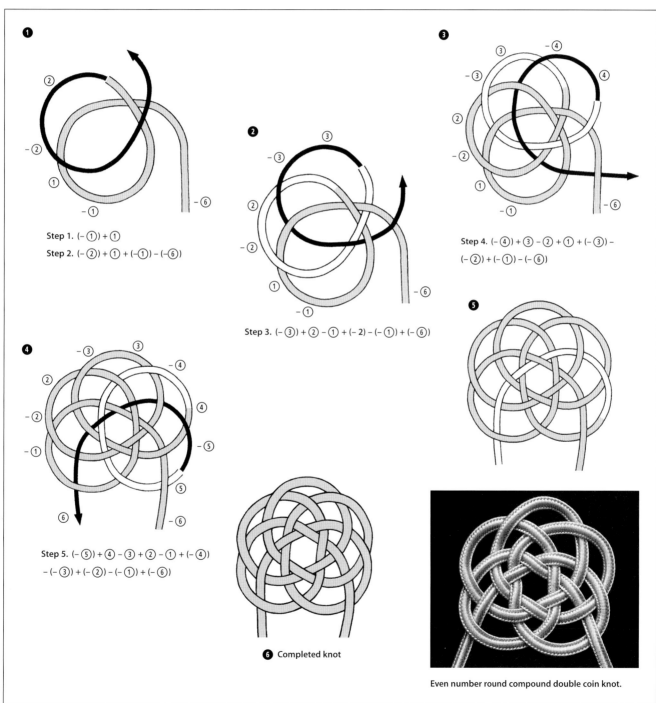

Step 1. (−①) + ①
Step 2. (−②) + ① + (−①) − (−⑥)

Step 3. (−③) + ② − ① + (− 2) − (−①) + (−⑥)

Step 4. (−④) + ③ − ② + ① + (−③) − (−②) + (−①) − (−⑥)

Step 5. (−⑤) + ④ − ③ + ② − ① + (−④) − (−③) + (−②) − (−①) + (−⑥)

❻ Completed knot

Even number round compound double coin knot.

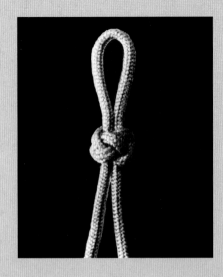

Button Knot

The fascinating little buttons found on traditional Chinese clothing, especially the openings of jackets, blouses, and dresses, are made from simple button knots. This knot is formed by overlapping two opposing outer loops, much like the double coin knot (page 106). Here, the right outer loop with the cord end beneath it is placed on top of the left outer loop. The right cord end is then woven clockwise around the overlapped layers. This knot does not lend itself to many variations.

Modified Knots

The knotting technique and the tightening process can be altered slightly to produce some modified knots. For example, the knotting process can be reversed, the knot body spread out and the four cord sections surrounding the knot body tied into four side knots. The knot body will make a 90-degree shift with a more pronounced three-dimensional effect. This modified knot is called the three-dimensional button knot.

Three-dimensional button
knot (see page 113).

Modified Knot Body

The basic knotting technique of the button knot can be changed to make both cord ends come out from two ends of the knot body so as to increase its applications. This modified knot is called the single cord end button knot.

Single cord end button
knot (see page 114).

Three-dimensional Button Knot

TYING INSTRUCTIONS

The knotting technique and the tightening process of a conventional button knot can be altered to produce this modified knot. To do so, reverse the knotting process, spread out the knot body and tie side knots on the four cord sections surrounding the knot body. The knot body will make a 90-degree shift and have a more pronounced 3D effect, making it suitable for incorporation in hanging ornaments.

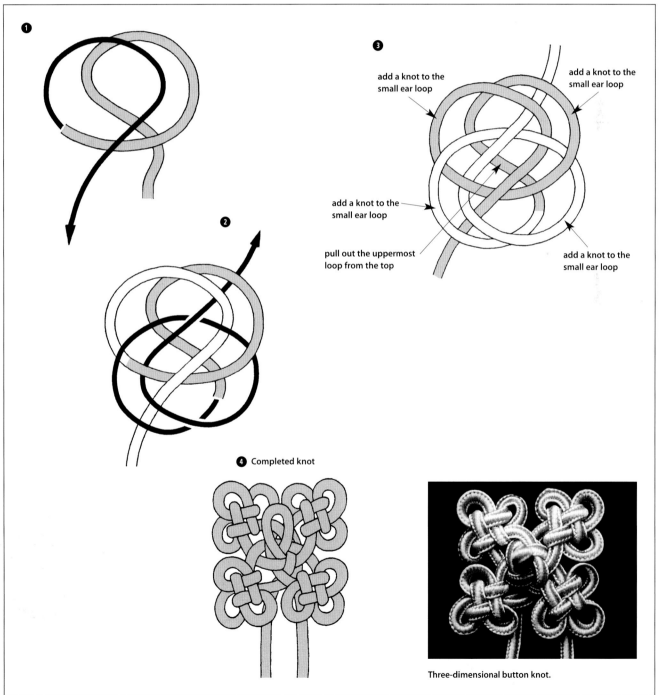

❸

add a knot to the small ear loop

add a knot to the small ear loop

add a knot to the small ear loop

pull out the uppermost loop from the top

add a knot to the small ear loop

❹ Completed knot

Three-dimensional button knot.

Single Cord End Button Knot

TYING INSTRUCTIONS

Step 1. Tie the right cord end into ear loop 1 in an anticlockwise direction. Tie ear loop 2 on top and overlap with 1. **Step 2.** Carry on anticlockwise with the right cord end. Pull through 1, pass over 2, pull through 1, pass over the left cord end and at the same time pull through 2 and 1 to complete the third ear loop. **Step 3.** Tighten the knot by pulling the two cord ends in opposite directions.

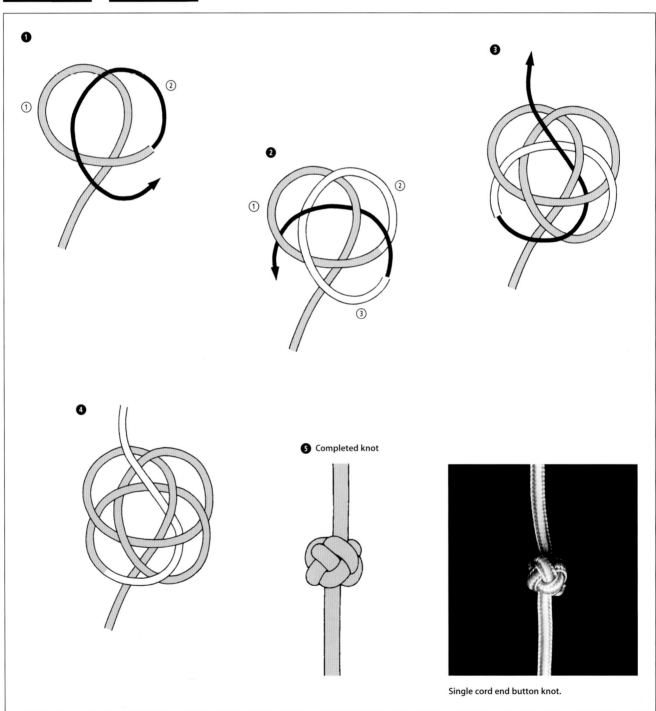

5 Completed knot

Single cord end button knot.

Creative Chinese Knotting Designs

Since the publication of her first book, *Chinese Knotting: Creative Designs That Are Easy and Fun!*, nearly twenty-five years ago, Lydia Chen has been relentless in her researches into Chinese knots. She has continued to explore the origins of Chinese knots by examining ancient artifacts and learning from their intricacy, and at the same time has continuously invented new knots and accumulated a vast personal collection of designs. The following section is a sampling of her creative knot formations.

In *Chinese Knotting* and her second book, *Fun with Chinese Knotting: Making Your Own Fashion Accessories and Accents*, detailed notes and diagrams were given for each knotting application. Here, however, because of the complexity of the new formations discussed, no diagrams are provided, only detailed descriptions and a photograph of each finished design. This has been done intentionally; the designs are primarily intended to inspire readers to create their own masterpieces.

The chapter is divided into six sections: (1) Conceiving a Design, (2) Real and Imaginary Creatures, (3) Flowers and People, (4) Painting Chinese Knots, (5) Plafond Designs and (6) Jewelry and Ornaments.

CONCEIVING A DESIGN

When you have a sound knowledge of the basic knotting techniques and such fundamentals as appropriate cord materials, choice of color, etc., and are ready to move on to more complex formations, it is advisable to start by copying other people's designs rather than trying to create your own. In this way, you can profit from any mistakes you make in the selection of cords or the amount of space you leave, say, for knots in an inner circle. It takes practice to get these things right. Moreover, when imitating other people's work, you can always make some modifications or add in knots of your own, such as side knots. You can then gradually move away from copying to creating your own designs. Here are some handy tips:

1. *Making a sketch*: It is important to start by making a sketch of the design you plan to do so that all the cords and knots will blend together harmoniously to produce a graceful and elegant work of art. Not only will a sketch make it easier for you to decide on the size of each of the knots and the density of the weave, but also to estimate the total cord length required. Ideas for subject matter can be derived from illustrations in books or on greeting cards, etc. but also from motifs found on Chinese ceramics, textiles, embroidery, carvings and paintings/scrolls.

2. *Choosing the correct cord*: Basically, thick cord is more suitable for fairly simple knots to achieve a sharp and forceful visual image. Thinner cords are more suitable for smaller, more intricate knots as they highlight the finer details. When a knot is used to embellish an ornament, it is important to choose cord that matches the size and grain of the ornament. For most designs, use cords of intermediate thickness.

3. *Estimating the required cord length*: The amount of cord needed for a design depends largely on the thickness of the cord. The thicker the cord, the greater the length required. To determine the length of cord needed for a particular knot formation, it is necessary to calculate the length required for each individual knot, then to add these up to get the total length. Alternatively, you can estimate the total length by doing a trial run by placing the cord on the sketch. The longer you work at knot formations, the more accurate your estimates will become.

4. *Estimating space in the center*: You also have to estimate the amount of space you need to leave for knots in an inner circle. Also the required length of cords for knots

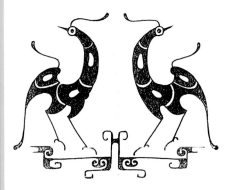

Sketch of a design.

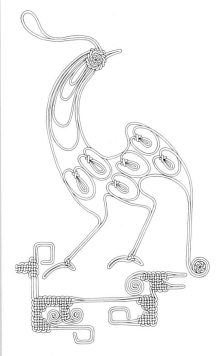

Knotted design using a cord of the desired thickness in the required length.

A balanced formation of closed and open spaces tied with an appropriate sized cord.

on the periphery, such as those on each side of a *hui ling* knot, needs to be calculated. Only then will you be able to create enough space to accommodate the knots in the inner circle of the formation.

5. *Knotting the inner and outer circles simultaneously*: Although it is possible to make a large knot formation with a single cord, this can be both tedious and inconvenient. When the appearance of a knot formation will not be compromised by using multiple knots, for example, when it is possible to hide loose cord ends inside the body of a knot formation, it is better to use multiple cords, especially when making fairly complex knots such as the *hui ling*. For this particular knot, it is easier to tie both the inner and outer circles simultaneously using two different cords. Similarly, when you have completed the three sides of a *pan chang* knot in the outer circle, you can use another cord to tie the fourth side. In this way, you can tie and tighten at the same time, which will not only save time but also the amount of cord material needed, not to mention the fact that the end product will be neater and more elegant.

6. *Knotting one or both ends of a single cord*: When tying small knots, especially those used to embellish ornaments, it is generally better to tie the main knot with both cord ends and the side knots with a single cord end. But for big knot formations, it is easier to tie with a single cord end and follow it through the knotting process; in this way, the two cord ends will not intertwine. You can also start tying from the center of the cord in one direction until completion, then use the other half of the same cord to tie in the opposite direction. This is a less messy and more convenient way to knot.

7. *Tightening and adjusting knots*: When tying a knot formaton on top of a sketch, it is advisable to pin plastic-headed board or map pins onto the sketch, placed on a piece of corkboard or a shallow cardboard box, as you go along to hold the knots in place and retain the shape. Adjust and tighten immediately after completing one section of the knot to avoid taking up too much space on the board. Also, by doing it this way, you will avoid losing some shared cords.

Completed knot formation.

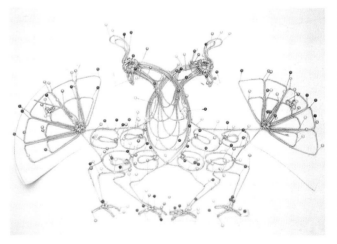

Using colorful board or map pins to hold a formation in place as it is tied.

Real and Imaginary Creatures

It is a challenge to use Chinese knots to project phoenix and other creatures, some real, others imaginary, that are found on early artifacts, or the flying maidens and dancers depicted in ancient wall paintings. Chinese knotting is limited in the sense that it cannot express itself as freely as painting or sculpture. It is very difficult, even with the best knotting technique, to express movement and life.

Ancient knitting artists sometimes remedied this situation by adding paint to their works. The author was thus inspired to do the same. In this section, in addition to presenting the best in Chinese knotting, some other techniques for adding life to the work are given in order to achieve the maximum impact.

1 Designs 1 and 2 are representations of phoenixes found on brassware from the Warring States Period. The bench on which the birds are perching in Design 1 is very typical of this period and makes the entire knot formation very lively and reminiscent of the times.

The big, round eyes and drooping tail in the original work can only be expressed by using the round brocade knot with compound outer loops. To show the majesty of the birds, tie double connection knots and embellish them with red cords to represent feathers.

TYING INSTRUCTIONS
1. Use the round brocade knot with compound outer loops to knot the head of each phoenix. The number of ear loops depends on the size of the phoenix's head and eyes plus the number of outer loops needed in the two sketches. Fourteen ear loops are used here. Wrap every second ear loop. The last cord end must come out from an appropriate part of the knot body.
2. Make the feathers by knotting numerous single loop double connection knots.
3. Make the claws from two clover leaf knots with two outer loops.
4. Knot the bench on which the birds are perching using the modified *pan chang* knotting technique.
5. Adjust and tighten the phoenixes' heads first, then knot and tighten each knot unit until completion. You can also tighten the whole formation after the entire design is completed, but in that case you would have to use a lot more cord during the knotting of the design.

2 Same knotting process as in Design 1.

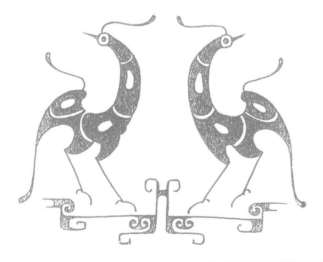

Phoenixes on a piece of brassware from the Warring States Period.

3 This design is adapted from a piece of jade from the Western Han Dynasty. The creatures resemble half parrots, half standing tigers. The emphasis is on the parrot-like beaks and the tiger-like protruding chests and abdomens. The double coin knot is highly appropriate in this case for producing the necessary curved and protruding effect.

TYING INSTRUCTIONS
1. For each parrot's head, tie a round brocade knot with compound outer knots, in this case sixteen. Wrap every fourth ear loop.
2. Make each body by knotting double coin knots with both cord ends. Adjust the cord density to project the body's protusion and curvature.
3. For the stand on which the creatures are resting, use a *pan chang* knot with compound outer loops and a modified *pan chang* knot.

A piece of jade from the Western Han Dynasty.

4 This design is adapted from a piece of Han Dynasty brassware. The necking birds represent a loving couple, hence the neck is the focus of the formation. But in order to make the knot as elegant as possible, the fanned tail also needs to be highlighted. A good luck knot with compound outer loops, enhanced with other colored cords, will produce this lavish effect.

TYING INSTRUCTIONS

1. For each head, claw and body, follow the knotting process in Design 1 (page 118).
2. For each tail, tie six ear loops, inclusive of both cord ends, into a good luck knot with compound outer loops.
3. After tightening, sew in the colored cords and hide the cord ends inside the knot body.
4. Make sure the necks of the bird are adjusted so that they are exactly the same length. If not, the intersections of all the outer loops will not fall on the same axis, thus affecting the overall appearance of the design.

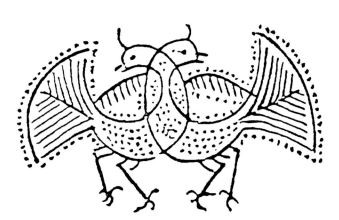

A bird design on a piece of Han Dynasty brassware.

5 & 6

Designs 5 and 6, adapted from a Han Dynasty stone carving, illustrate a phoenix flaunting its wings. Its fluttering cockscomb, protruding chest, outspread wings, inward-pointing claws and slightly pointed tail contribute to a sense of calm in motion.

TYING INSTRUCTIONS

1. Tie a *hui ling* knot with compound outer loops for the head and cockscomb. Tie the exterior outer loops into double connection knots and pull the interior outer loops through these knots.
2. Leave a suitable length of left cord, then tie the left wing using a *pan chang* knot with reduced cords and a creeper knot. Tie a cloverleaf knot and a double connection knot for its claw.
3. Leave a suitable length of right cord and repeat Step 2 with the right cord to form the right wing and claw.
4. Use the cord in the middle to tie a long double connection knot. Weave the rest of the cord along the abdomen, then hide the cord ends inside the knot body.
5. For the tail, tie a *pan chang* knot and a *lingzhi* knot. The tail should not be too heavy but at the same time be pointed to show the bird's vigor.

A phoenix on a Han Dynasty stone carving.

7 This phoenix design is adapted from a Northern Wei stone carving. It depicts a phoenix about to take flight or coming in to rest. The curves on the bottom part of the tail indicate fluttering feathers.

TYING INSTRUCTIONS

1. Tie a *hui ling* knot with compound outer loops for the head, as in Designs 5 and 6, but tighten the knot from the back, not the front. Lengthen two outer loops to form the cockscomb. To form the tongue, make one more round of the outer loop that forms the beak.
2. Leave a suitable length of the outer loop on the left side of the neck. Arrange in a curving line to form the neck, then tie the left wing using a creeper knot and a modified *pan chang* knot. Take the cord directly to the end of the tail.
3. Leave a suitable length of the outer loop on the right side of the neck, form the outline of the neck, then tie the right wing using a creeper knot and a modified *pan chang* knot. Pull the rest of the cord to form the outline of the abdomen and curved outline at the bottom of the tail.
4. Use the four central cords to tie, first, a long double coin knot and, secondly, a compound double coin knot for the body. Weave one of the four cord ends directly to the tail end, and the second one to the tail and tie a cloverleaf knot. Tie the last one into the body, then pull it to the tail end.
5. Tie a button knot with a single cord for each knee, and a cloverleaf knot and a double connection knot for each claw.

8 This peculiar animal, with its bird's head, dragon's body and tiger's legs and tail, is adapted from a design on a copper mirror from the Warring States Period. Make sure the curvature of both tails projects balance and grace.

TYING INSTRUCTIONS

1. Tie a round brocade knot with compound outer loops for the head. Sixteen loops are used here. Wrap every second ear loop. After tightening the knot, pull the cord ends out from the neck and dig out another cord in the head (or lengthen the loop between the two cord ends to make a broken line) to give four cord ends.

2. Tie the four cord ends into a compound double coin knot for the body. Play around with the cord density to achieve the best possible curvature. Fold the cords in the leg to form the knee.

The design on a copper mirror from the Warring States Period.

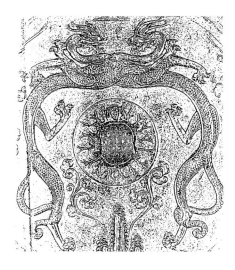

The design on a copper mirror from the Tang Dynasty.

9 This double dragon and tortoise design is adapted from a Tang Dynasty copper mirror. The dragons' bodies are made from a series of variously woven double coin knots.

TYING INSTRUCTIONS

1. See pages 68–9, *Chinese Knotting: Creative Designs That Are Easy and Fun!* for instructions on making a dragon's head. Tie the head twice to make it bigger. Tie the outer loops into double coin knots to form the horn. Use a single cord to tie the neck.

2. Use other cords to tie a broad double coin knot to make the rest of the body above the tail. At a suitable place, pull out a single cord end and tie a long double coin knot for each paw. Tie a round brocade knot to make the claws.

3. To form the shell of the tortoise, tie a *pan chang* knot as hexagonal knots with reduced cords.

10 This scene of a fighting cock is adapted from a wall painting in China's famous Dunhuang Caves. The lowered neck, long stride, upward-pointing posterior claws and pointed tail all indicate a fighting stance.

TYING INSTRUCTIONS

1. Tie a round brocade knot with eighteen outer loops to make the head. Wrap every second ear loop. Pull the cord ends out from the back of the neck.
2. To make the body and tail, tie a single cord end into a *pan chang* knot with reduced cords. Alternatively, tie a *pan chang* knot with reduced cords together with a cord end for making both feet. It is best to lay out the design first on a board, anchoring the cord with pins before tying, for better control of the knot formation.

A scene of fighting cocks from a Dunhuang wall painting.

12 This design is not based on any particular flying maiden at Dunhuang. Rather, it has been created purely to show the graceful downward flight and the fluttering tassels of the maidens. The two are differentiated by the varying length and arch of their eyebrows.

TYING

1. To make the headdress of each maiden, tie a round brocade knot with seventeen outer loops, in which every sixth loop is wrapped, and a *hui ling* knot.
2. Tie a double coin knot and a *pan chang* knot with compound outer loops for the breasts; a modified *pan chang* knot for each dress; a long double coin knot for each earring; and a double coin knot for each bracelet.

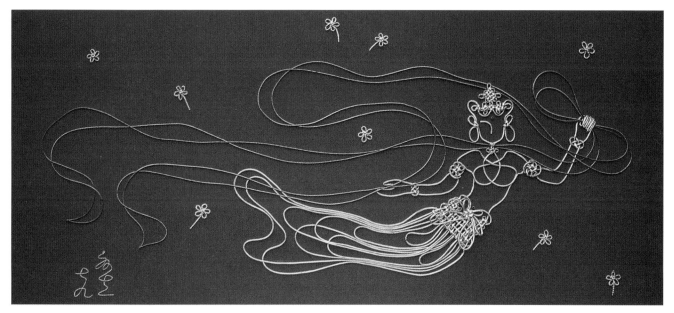

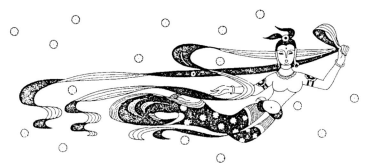

A *fei tian* in a wall mural at China's Dunhuang Caves.

11 *Fei tian*, literally "flying maidens," are also known as celestial beings and *apsara* in Buddhism. They appear as divine dancers and musicians adorning statuary, paintings and temple structures. According to a Buddhist scripture, *fei tian* were born as lotuses in the Holy Pond. Whenever the Buddha preached, they would hover in the sky, play music or sprinkle flowers, their long, golden tassel-like costumes swaying gracefully in the wind.

Of the nearly 500 cave-temples at Dunhuang in China, 270 feature *fei tian* in their mural paintings, covering a period from the fourth to the eleventh centuries. More than 4,500 of these paintings can be seen on the tops of alcoves, around borders and surrounding the preaching Buddhas.

The *fei tian* in the design above does not imitate any particular one in Dunhuang. The sudden ascent of the *fei tian* and her serpentine tassels are used merely to portray speed and a sense of unfettered freedom.

TYING INSTRUCTIONS
1. Tie a round brocade knot to make the hair bun.
2. After completing the head, lay out the design on a board, anchoring the cord with pins.
3. Tie a double coin knot to make the breasts of the maiden and a *pan chang* knot with compound outer loops for the lower body.

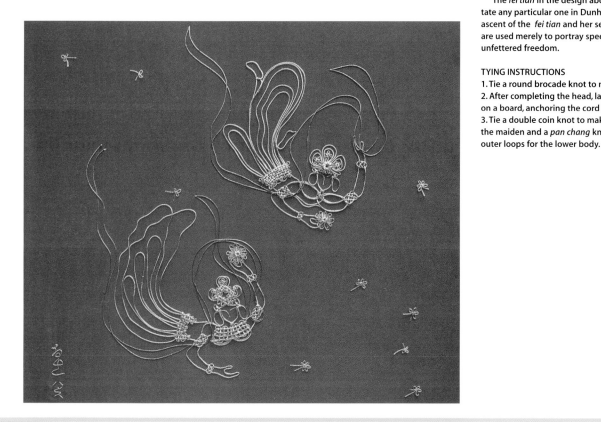

13 The Mogao Grottoes in China's Dunhuang Caves contain probably the world's most extraordinary gallery of Buddhist art: paintings, sculptures, Buddhist scriptures, historical documents, textiles and other relics. Included are not only paintings of *fei tian* flying maidens but also of the dance goddess, no doubt based on dancers in the palace at the time. In this knot formation, the lithe movements of the dancers and their fluttering shawls are convincingly depicted.

TYING INSTRUCTIONS

1. Tie a *pan chang* knot with compound outer loops and a cloverleaf knot with two outer loops in a loop-sharing fashion to make the hair bun, and a cloverleaf knot to make the rest of the hair.
2. Tie double coin knots to make the upper body. Use broad double coin knots for the upper arm bands and double coin knots for the bracelets.
3. Tie a left and a right *pan chang* knot with compound outer loops to make the lower body. Bend the loops to represent the feet and the fluttering skirt and shawls. Lastly, unite both cord ends just beneath the navel and tie into a cloverleaf knot.

14 Again, this knot creation is not based on any particular dancer in Dunhuang's wall murals. Rather, it reflects the author's wish to capture the graceful movement of the dancer, with emphasis on her dress and her fluttering shawl.

TYING INSTRUCTIONS
1. Tie a round brocade knot with sixteen outer loops, in which every sixth loop is wrapped, and the same with overlapped loops to form the headdress.
2. Tie a double coin knot for the breasts; a modified *pan chang* knot with twenty ear loops, every ninth loop wrapped, to make the dress; a long double coin knot for the upper arm band; and a double coin knot for the bracelet.
3. Use a different colored cord to make the shawl.

Flowers and People

Because of the limitations of Chinese knotting in terms of expressing flexibility and movement, it is not easy, though not impossible, to form flowers and people. Success with knotting flowers depends very much on the type of knots used. Although you may think that a chrysanthemum is readily formed from a round brocade knot with multiple outer loops and a compound good luck knot, this is not necessarily the case as these are not very versatile knots.

When making knots depicting people, it is sometimes necessary to realign the cords in order to better express the limbs.

15 This "still life" of a vase of wild flowers is an innovative interpretation of the traditional sketch or painting. It is tied with jute cords.

TYING INSTRUCTIONS
1. To make the vase, tie a cloverleaf knot and tighten the loop to form the mouth. Leave a cord end on the right side to complete the right part of the vase. Pull the other cord end out of the knot body to the left to complete the left part of the vase. Tie a long *pan chang knot* to make the base.
2. For the flowers, tie round brocade knots, then pull the cord ends back to the knot body to make the center of the flowers.
3. Tie *pan chang knot*s with compound outer loops for the leaves.

16 This bouquet of chrysanthemums is also tied with jute cords. The size of the flowers and leaves should be varied to make the bouquet look as realistic as possible. Use finer cords to tie the dragonfly so that it also looks in proportion to the bouquet.

TYING INSTRUCTIONS
1. For each flower, tie a good luck knot with compound outer loops, with the small outer loops placed inside the bigger ones to produce a double petal effect. Hide both cord ends inside the knot body, break up the cords to form the centers of the flower. Vary the number of ear loops in every wrap in order to change the size of the central hole.
2. Make the leaves from *pan chang knots*.
3. See the instructions on page 70, *Chinese Knotting: Creative Designs That Are Easy and Fun!*, for the knotting of the dragonfly.

17 That just the right knots have been chosen to create the sunflowers in this display is obvious from the three-dimensional effect achieved by the seeds encased in petals.

TYING INSTRUCTIONS
1. Tie a good luck knot with multiple compound outer loops to make up the required number of petals. The central hole created is ideal for containing the *pan chang knot* with reduced cords as it resembles a pistil filled with seeds.
2. Tie a *pan chang knot* with reduced cords to make the pistil of the flower.
3. Tie *pan chang knot*s with compound outer loops to make the leaves.

18 These knotted dancers were inspired by the little figures frequently seen in children's drawings.

TYING INSTRUCTIONS
1. Tie a cloverleaf knot to make the ribbon on the head followed by a round brocade knot for the face. Then pull the cord ends upwards through the knot body and tie another cloverleaf knot to make the hair. The outer loop of this knot then becomes the arm. (When tying the second dancer, make sure you tie the cord together with the out-stretched arm of the first dancer, then only tie the cloverleaf knot below the face of the second dancer.)
2. Tie a modified *pan chang knot* to make the dress. Break up the cord on the skirt bottom to give a hula dance effect
3. Tie each cord end into a foot, then hide it inside the dancer's body.
4. Tie a single cord end into a *lingzhi* knot on top of the dancers to form a canopy. Make sure that the front and back of the knot are identical.

Painting Chinese Knots

Traditionally, Chinese knots are made of soft materials although hard materials such as wire are now being incorporated into ultra modern designs. Author Lydia Chen has introduced the concept of combining Chinese knots with painting techniques in order to achieve sculpture-like results. She coats her painted knots with shellac and then buffs them to attain the combined elegance of knot and paint artistry.

PAINT ART ON CHINESE KNOTS

From archaeological records, it is known that painting using tree sap began as long ago as 5000 BCE. Paint provides a long-lasting protective effect and beautifies a coated object.

There are various types of paint arts, but here it is sufficient to simply coat finished Chinese knots to stiffen and protect them, as well as to add a different dimension to the art of Chinese knotting. When coating Chinese knots with paint, care must be taken with the following:

1. *Cord material:* It is better to paint thick cords rather than thin ones. Because of the bigger space created between adjoining cords when using thin cords, the paint tends to make the cords stick together. Loose cords, due to the uneven absorption of paints, tend to have a pocked appearance. Even in the case of tight formations, it is importamt to minimize folding in order to avoid an uneven shine.

2. *Paint thickness:* The technique of applying paint to cords is similar to painting items made from bamboo and rattan. The artist's objective will determine the thickness and number of coats to be applied. But be aware that the appearance of the knot will change with every layer of coat applied. Generally, only a few coats are necessary.

3. *Painting overlapping areas:* Be extra careful with the paint thickness on overlapped areas. It is best to slightly separate the overlap to allow optimum absorption of the paint. If the amount of paint is inadequate, the cords in the overlap will be glaringly exposed. If there is excessive paint, the accumulation of it on the overlap will make it look dull. Also, the artist should ensure every part of the knot is painted to avoid any bare cords when the finished work is viewed from different angles

4. *Buffing overlapping areas:* Take special care when buffing overlaps. It is advisable to always separate each overlap during the coating process. If, for whatever reason, this cannot be done, make sure the paint thickness on the overlap is adjusted during the coating and buffing process.

19 This is a tight knot made from cord materials with a pronounced grain. A thin coat of paint highlights the grain.

TYING INSTRUCTIONS
1. Tie the seven ear loops, including both cord ends, into a cloverleaf knot. Use the press two technique on the ear loops to knot the first layer of a good luck knot.
2. On the back of the knot body, lengthen the small outer loops in a clockwise fashion, then use the press two technique on the ear loops to knot the second layer of the good luck knot.
3. Apply an appropriate number of coats of paint.

20 Use different color paints to coat this work and break the tradition of a single color knot tied with a single color cord.

TYING INSTRUCTIONS
1. Tie a cotton cord into a 90-degree shiftweave *pan chang knot* using the two up, two down type of over-lapped outer loops.
2. Paint the knot with three different colors until the grain is barely visible, then apply appropriate coats of shellac.

21 This good luck knot wall decoration is embellished with traditional Chinese red paint and silver and gold flakes.

TYING INSTRUCTIONS

1. Use a thick cotton cord to tie the *ji* good luck character (top portion) and the ram's head.
2. Apply shellac followed by Chinese red paint.
3. When the paint is dry, apply silver and gold flakes on the knot, then apply another thin coat of shellac.

23 The knot depicts a lotus in the shape of a *ru yi* scepter. It is adapted from the Manjusri Bodhisattva painting discovered in Shanxi Province.

TYING INSTRUCTIONS

1. Tie a cloverleaf knot and a *pan chang* knot to make the head of the *ru yi*.
2. Pull the cords to form the shaft and tie them into a double coin knot to form the end portion of the *ru yi*.
3. Ensure that the lotus petals are of different lengths and that the end portion of the *ru yi* is properly curved.
4. Apply paint. Make sure that the cord ends are glued tightly by the paint.

22 In order to give a real sense of sculpture to this work, additional coats of paint are applied to completely cover the grain of the cord material.

TYING INSTRUCTIONS

1. Tie a thick cotton cord into a *lingzhi* knot. Tie each cord end into a flat knot, and hide the cord end inside an overlap.
2. Apply sufficient coats of paint to cover the grain. Ensure that the cord ends are glued firmly to the knot with the paint.

24

As in Design 20, use different color paints on this knot to break the tradition of a single color cord making a single color knot. In addition to the different colors, the focus is on the central bottom layer, where a different color is just perceptible peeping through.

TYING INSTRUCTIONS
1. Use four ear loops, including both cord ends, to tie the first layer of a good luck knot.
2. Lengthen clockwise the small outer loops on the back of the knot body, then, also clockwise, press every second small outer loop into the subsequent one.
3. Apply three different color paints to the knot until the grain is barely visible, then apply appropriate coats of shellac.

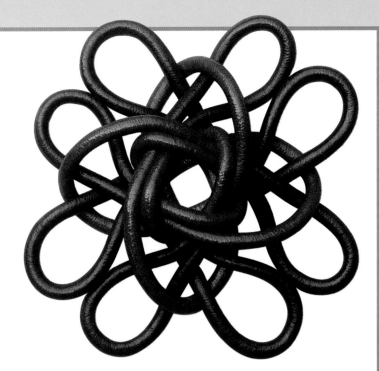

25

This knot is finished using the laborious technique of traditional paint art.

TYING INSTRUCTIONS
1. Tie a thick cotton cord into a *lingzhi* knot, then tie one cord end into a cloverleaf knot and unite both cord ends at the back of the knot body.
2. Apply paint until the grain is barely visible. Ensure that both cord ends are sealed together by the paint.
3. Apply gold flakes.

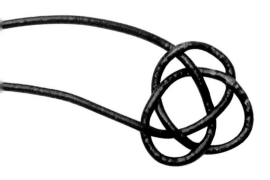

26

The two layers are purposely separated in this work in order to highlight the 3D sculpture effect.

TYING INSTRUCTIONS
1. Combining the knotting techniques of the *pan chang* knot with overlapped outer loops and the shiftweave *pan chang* knot, tie a thick cotton cord with four ear loops on each side into three separate units of *pan chang* knots. The middle knot should have a one up, one down 180-degree shift, while the other two, a two up, two down 180-degree shift.
2. Apply paint. Because the formation is very loosely knotted, the bottom layer is clearly visible. This layer should therefore be painted carefully.

27

TYING INSTRUCTIONS

1. Use two different color cords. Split into four groups and tie a central round brocade knot with 24 ear loops, wrapping every fifth loop.
2. Use the two cord ends from every cord section to tie a round brocade knot. Then tie each outer loop into a cloverleaf knot to form the second layer.
3. For the outermost circle, tie the orange and yellow cord ends into button knots, then arrange the remaining cords in a semicircle around the knot body and hide the cord ends inside it.

The word "plafond" refers to any flat, vaulted or domed ceiling, especially one having some painted or stucco ornamentation. The ceilings often have a circular design in the center with repeating patterns, often in clearly defined segments, radiating out to the edges of bordering rectangles. Such ceilings were common lining the verandas and staterooms of ancient Chinese palaces. As its name suggests, the plafond knot has a central focal point, usually containing an auspicious motif, with other knots radiating symmetrically in all directions.

28

TYING INSTRUCTIONS

1. Tie a purple and a green cord into a round brocade knot with 72 ear loops, wrapping every second loop.
2. Tie the purple cord into two loops with sufficient length to be used as broken cords to tie the outer circle (see step 5 below).
3. Then tie the green cord into two ear loops, a cloverleaf knot, three ear loops, a round brocade knot, three ear loops, a cloverleaf knot and finally two ear loops as one single unit. Pull the green cord into the inner circle, complete another unit and pull out (see step 6 below).
4. Use the purple cord to tie a second unit.
5. *Tying the outer circle*: Cut the purple outer loop, then tie both cord ends into a double connection knot, a cloverleaf knot, a *pan chang* knot and a cloverleaf knot respectively. Separate the two cord ends and tie a double connection knot followed by a cloverleaf knot with a single cord end, then tie this cord and that from an adjacent unit into a double connection knot and a button knot. Then tie a cloverleaf knot with a single cord end and hide all the cord ends inside the button knot.

6. *Tying the inner circle*: To tie a single unit, first tie half a double connection knot, half a cloverleaf knot and half a button knot, then turn back the cord end, leave an outer loop and carry on knotting a *ru yi* knot and a double connection knot. When knotting the last unit in the inner circle, use the "single cord end and it must come out from somewhere else" technique to tie a button knot. Then tie a cloverleaf knot with multiple outer loops to form a hexagon. Finally, pull the cord through the button knot and complete the entire unit.

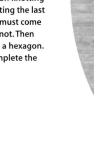

29

TYING INSTRUCTIONS

1. Use a portion of four different color cords to tie a round brocade knot with 64 outer ear loops. Wrap every fourth loop.
2. Use the coffee color cord to do the outer circle. Use the green cord to tie another round brocade knot in the inner circle. Hence these two cords must be longer.
3. See page 27 for the knotting technique.

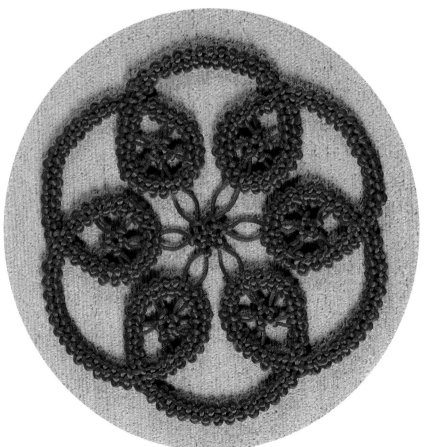

30

This design comprises a hollow and revolving modified *pan chang* knot. First lay out the design on a piece of chipboard or a shallow cardboard box, then estimate the total number of ear loops and the central space required. The latter must be big enough to accommodate the inner knots so that upon tightening they will look neither too loose nor too dense.

TYING INSTRUCTIONS

1. Tie according to the design using the modified *pan chang* knotting technique. Take special care with the revolving portions. It is faster and less messy to first arrange the long sides of the *pan chang* knot on the board, then concurrently knot the inner and outer circle with two separate cords.
2. Tie a constellation knot within each of the six "water droplets."
3. Make a compound brocade knot in the center.

31 The whole purpose of this knot is to display the knotting technique of the good luck knot with compound outer loops. Make the knot with two different color cords for added variation.

TYING INSTRUCTIONS
1. Tie a pink and a red cord into a good luck knot with compound outer loops. Ensure that the pink cord forms the outer circle and tie a cloverleaf knot on every loop. There are eighteen ear loops in all, including both cord ends. Press every third ear loop in the first layer, and every third ear loop in the second layer.
2. Lengthen the red outer loops in the outermost circle. Cut each loop and tie both cord ends into a double connection knot and a *lingzhi* knot.

32 This complex design work is quite labor-intensive. Moreover, tightening the knot so that the cords are arranged properly is a challenge and needs to be done very carefully so that the final appearance is neat and tidy.

TYING INSTRUCTIONS
1. First tie a red cord into twelve double connection knots and round compound double connection knots.
2. Tie a silver cord into a bat design and continue weaving these along the double coin and round compound double coin knots on the outer edge. A large number of silver cords is needed. Hide the connections inside the bats.

33

TYING INSTRUCTIONS

1. Tie three different color cords together into a round brocade knot with 64 outer loops. Wrap every fourth loop. Use the yellow cord to tie the outer circle. (A large quantity of yellow cord is needed.)
2. Break the yellow outer loop. Note that the breaking point is not at the center. If the breaking point of the first lotus petal is left short and the right longer (so short that it can be hidden inside the knot body), then the breaking point of the second petal should be left short and the right long. Tie the longer cord ends from both petals from inside out into a double connection knot. Pull the cord ends at the back towards the left and right, and tie each cord end with that from a neighboring cord from inside out into a double connection knot until the whole knot formation is completed.

34 This design is tied using the knotting technique of a shiftweave *pan chang* knot sharing an outer loop with a cloverleaf knot with two outer loops. The main central knot is the shiftweave *pan chang* knot. The outer circle is formed by tying double connection knots using the technique of ear loop sharing, to create a square formation. The entire knot formation looks like a leaf of the pyrus plant. The design can be tightened into different shapes according to one's fancy.

TYING INSTRUCTIONS

1. Use both cord ends to start tying from the central major cloverleaf knot. Tie a 180-degree shiftweave one up, one down type of *pan chang* knot and pull the cord away from the central knot.
2. In the center of the four sides of the *pan chang* knot, tie a side knot composed of four cloverleaf knots with two outer loops by the loop-sharing technique. Tie a cloverleaf knot with three outer loops on the join of two of these cloverleaf knots, and also, during this process, tie with neighboring outer loops into a double coin knot.

35 This creation is a display of the shiftweave *pan chang* knotting technique. The rest of the knot is tied with double cords which highlight the shiftweave portion in the central knot.

TYING INSTRUCTIONS
1. Arrange the cords according to the design on a piece of chipboard or a shallow cardboard box. Pay particular attention to shared cords.
2. Start by tying a cloverleaf knot. Upon reaching the *pan chang* knot body with a 90-degree shift, weave another round in the shiftweave portion and tie a side knot on each outer loop.

36 The central part of this design is made by combining the knotting techniques of the shiftweave *pan chang* knot and the *pan chang* good luck knot.

TYING INSTRUCTIONS
1. First, tie a *pan chang* good luck knot. When the cord ends reach the center, use the 90-degree one up, one down shifweave *pan chang* knotting technique to tie the first layer of a *pan chang* good luck knot.
2. Along the outer edge, use a single cord end to tie four *ru yi* knots and four *pan chang* good luck knots.
3. Finally, use the *pan chang* good luck knotting technique to tie a second layer of *pan chang* good luck knots.

37 This work is formed by a shiftweave *pan chang* knot with two groups of different color knots along the outer border tied using the loop-sharing technique.

TYING INSTRUCTIONS
1. Tie a purple cord into a 180-degree shiftweave one up, one down type of *pan chang* knot.
2. Tie four separate red cords into four cloverleaf knots with two outer loops by sharing the loops, and link up the double coin knot with the outer loop of the major knot.
3. Tie four separate pink cords into four cloverleaf knots with two outer loops by sharing the loops, then link them up with the red knot formation by sharing loops.

38 This knot is done by combining the techniques of the shiftweave *pan chang* knot and the *pan chang* good luck knot, with four rams' heads along the periphery.

TYING INSTRUCTIONS
1. Tie the first layer of the *pan chang* good luck knot using the 180-degree shiftweave one up, one down *pan chang* knotting technique.
2. Weave along the periphery and tie a ram's head with a single cord end.
3. Finally, tie the second layer of the central major knot using the *pan chang* good luck knotting technique.

39 This knot formation is made by combining the techniques of the *pan chang* knot with compound outer loops, the shiftweave *pan chang* knot and the *pan chang* good luck knot.

TYING INSTRUCTIONS
1. Use five ear loops on each side to tie a shift-weave *pan chang* good luck knot with compound outer loops, with four groups of 180-degree shift, the central two groups one up, one down, and the top and bottom groups two up, two down.
2. Tie the second layer using the ordinary *pan chang* good luck knotting technique.
3. Tie each corner loop into a good luck knot with four outer loops using the pull and wrap technique, then tie each outer loop of the good luck knot into a cloverleaf knot.

40 This knot formation is done by combining the techniques of the *pan chang* knot with compound outer loops, the shiftweave *pan chang* knot and the *hui ling* knot.

TYING INSTRUCTIONS
1. Use six ear loops on each side to tie a shift-weave *pan chang* knot with overlapped loops, with three groups of 180-degree shift, one up, one down and two up, two down, to surround the *hui ling* knot which is right at the center.
2. Adjust and tighten to stress the central shift-weave pattern. The hollow spaces within the knot formation lend more decorative value.

41 Although this is a time-consuming and painstaking knot formation, the characters in the work provide a splendid display of the knotting technique of the modified *pan chang* knot at its best.

TYING INSTRUCTIONS
1. Use a single cord to tie a series of *lingzhi* knots to form a decorative outer circle.
2. Lay out the characters in the center first on a board, then only knot them. Take special care with the sharing and conjoining cord sections among the squares and between the upper body (triangle) of the figures and the head.

42 This beautiful design is made by using modified polygonal *pan chang* knots with hollow centers to create two overlapping squares on the outside and a vacant space in the knot center to accommodate all incoming cords.

TYING INSTRUCTIONS
1. To avoid getting into a mess when knotting the modified *pan chang* knots with hollow centers, it is essential to lay out the design first.
2. Upon reaching two bends on the outer circle, take another cord and start knotting the inner circle. Upon completing three of the eight petal-shaped sides, take another cord to knot the innermost circle. Tighten this part first, then carry on with the rest. This tactic will help to avoid confusion and a messy result.

43 This work combines round brocade knots and rams' heads to form an elegant plafond design which stresses the planar nature of the four outer loops of both the big and the small round brocade knots.

TYING INSTRUCTIONS

1. Use 32 ear loops to make the big central round broacde knot, with every eight loops forming a single unit.

2. On each unit, tie a ram's head followed by a round brocade knot with six outer loops. Then, on one of these outer loops, tie a butterfly-like round brocade knot followed by a round brocade knot with six outer loops.

3. After completing one of the ram's head units, pull the cord end within and make a round, forming an ear loop for the knotting of the inner round brocade knot.

44 The main focus of this design is the change in the weave in the side knots, both inside and outside each corner loop of the *hui ling* knot.

TYING INSTRUCTIONS

1. With both cord ends, tie four cloverleaf knots with two outer loops and shared adjacent loops using the wrap one, pull one technique.

2. Use twelve ear loops on each side to tie a *hui ling* knot. Tie a cloverleaf knot on the second, sixth and tenth outer loops on each side, and a cloverleaf knot with two outer loops on the fourth and eighth loops and also the corner loop on each side. Notice the inner corner of the *hui ling* knot has a 180-degree two up, two down shift.

3. The central outer loop involves two up, two down interlocking.

45 This semi-3D plafond is designed with one side flat for framing purposes.

TYING INSTRUCTIONS
1. For each corner, tie a single unit comprising a cloverleaf knot, a 3D button knot (with a cloverleaf knot on the left, right and top parts of the knot), a double connection knot, a cloverleaf knot and a double connection knot respectively.
2. The major knot here is the *hui ling* knot with twelve ear loops on each side. Then, on each side of the *hui ling* knot, tie in this order: For the first outer loop, a cloverleaf knot, and on the second outer loop, a cloverleaf knot tied together with the outer loop from the cloverleaf knot on the abovementioned 3D button knot. Lengthen the fourth outer loop and tie a cloverleaf knot with two outer loops, together with the outer loop from the inner circle round brocade knot. Then the sixth outer loop, a cloverleaf knot. Lengthen the eighth outer loop and tie a cloverleaf knot with two outer loops, together with the outer loop from the inner circle round brocade knot. Tie outer loop ten together with the outer loop from the button knot into a cloverleaf knot with two outer loops followed by a cloverleaf knot.
3. There are nine ear loops on each inner side on this *hui ling* knot. Tie a cloverleaf knot on each corner. Lengthen the third and seventh ear loops on each side in preparation for the knotting of the round brocade knot in the innermost circle.
4. Together with the round brocade knot in the innermost circle, tie each of the two reserved loops on each inner side of the *hui ling* knot into two ear loops so that the outer loop in the center and that on the outer circle are tied into a cloverleaf knot with two outer loops.

46 This elegant design is formed using a modified *pan chang* knot to allow adequate space to accommodate all incoming cords to the center.

TYING INSTRUCTIONS
1. Tie a modified *pan chang* knot on the outside. Tie a *lingzhi* knot in each of the slots, but tighten its outer loops as small as possible.
2. Knot inwards from each corner, with the knots tied in this order: a shiftweave *pan chang* knot with a 90-degree shift, a cloverleaf knot, four cloverleaf knots with their two outer loops shared. Leave a long enough outer loop to tie the central round brocade knot.
3. Leave an outer loop in the center of the inner side of the slot, but remember to tie a cloverleaf knot first.
4. When knotting the last central outer loop, tie the first three outer loops from each corner and the center of each side into the round brocade knot in the inner circle. Wrap every second ear loop.

47 This design originates from the double diamond knot. It is an excellent example of the knotting technique of the *pan chang* knot with a hollow center, i.e. the *hui ling* knot. Within every pan *pan chang* with a hollow center, the knotting technique of the *pan chang* knot with compound/overlapped outer loops can be used to create a beautiful design.

TYING INSTRUCTIONS
1. Lay out the design on a board and anchor the cords with pins to avoid mixing up the shared ear loops.
2. Since this is a big design, tying with a single knot can be slow and tedious. It is best to tie simultaneously with different cords as well as tighten the knot formation section by section to save both time and cords. Also, you will not have to use so many board pins.
3. Start with the top left section of the *hui ling* knot. Use a different cord for the inner and outer sides of the knot. Cut a longer cord to tie the outer part of the

knot. Unite both the left and right cord ends after completing the small *hui ling* knot and a certain section of the big outer *hui ling* knot. Upon completion of the first *hui ling* knot, pull the ends of the cord on the inner side into the interior of the big *hui ling* knot, and use the two cord ends to separately complete the inner side of the big *hui ling* knot and the outer side of the small *hui ling* knot. Finally, unite both cord ends in the bottom left small *hui ling* knot to completely weave the inner side.
4. Take another cord to tie the inner side of the top right small *hui ling* knot and pull the rest of the cord into the interior of the big *hui ling* knot. Use both cord ends to separately complete the inner side of the big *hui ling* knot and the outer side of the small *hui ling* knot on the right side. Finally, pull both cord ends into the bottom right small *hui ling* knot and tie its inner side, then unite both cords.
5. Finally, take another cord and complete the three small *hui ling* knots on the left, right and center.

48 This design links three *hui ling* knots by combining the knotting technique of the *hui ling* knot, the shiftweave *pan chang* knot and the compound brocade knot. This knot formation has a unique tightening process.

TYING INSTRUCTIONS
1. Tie three linked *hui ling* knots and four groups of one up, one down 180-degree shiftweave *pan chang* knots.
2. Use the outer loops inside the big *hui ling* knot to tie a compound round brocade knot using the technique of wrapping every four ear loops and pulling the ear loops forward to wrap the next loop.
3. Within the interior of each of the two smaller *hui ling* knots, tie a two up, two down 180-degree shiftweave *pan chang* knot.

49 Besides displaying the hollow *pan chang* knot, i.e. the *hui ling* knot, and the solid *pan chang* knot, the design here also emphasizes the unique arrangement of the outer loops within the *hui ling* knots. Take special care in the ratio of the hollow and solid *pan chang* knots and the size of the inner space for the unique arrangement of the outer loops.

TYING INSTRUCTIONS
1. Tie two linked *hui ling* knots and tie each corner into a round brocade knot with thirteen outer loops, wrapping every fourth loop. Ensure that the over-lapped outer loops are all on the front or on the back.
2. Use four outer loops on each inner side of the *hui ling* knot to tie the central *pan chang* knot. Tie according to the draft layout where the outer loops have already been properly arranged.

Jewelry and Ornaments

The popularity of using Chinese knots for personal adornment and as accents on other items in daily use and in the home has reached an all-time time. In *Fun with Chinese Knotting: Making Your Own Fashion Accessories and Accents*, Lydia Chen introduced knotters to 135 practical knot formations employing a variety of cord materials and color combinations. In this book, she takes jewelry and home decor to new heights by focusing on the use of gold and silver cords to create exquisite necklace and earring sets as well as ornamental hanging formations.

Knotting with gold and silver cords requires thought, care and patience, but the end results are often stunning. Gold cords, being very fine, can get lost if a design is too complicated. Moreover, gold, being a highly reflective material, can be hard on a knotter's eyes.

The silver threads in silver cords must also be treated carefully, otherwise they will unravel and snap easily. It is also important when working with silver cords to tighten each section immediately after tying. Since silver cord can only be twisted and not bent repeatedly, it is necessary to calculate where the bends will fall so that there is not excessive bending – and breakage – during the tightening process.

50

TYING INSTRUCTIONS

1. Using both cord ends, tie a modified *pan chang* knot with a hollow center. Start with the cloverleaf knot at the top. Upon completion of three sets (right, left and center) of outer loops on the outer side, take another cord and start knotting from the center. This simultaneous knotting technique saves time and avoids getting the cord sections mixed up.
2. Use a similar but thicker cord to tie the necklace loop.

51

TYING INSTRUCTIONS

1. Using a single cord end, tie a modified *pan chang* knot with a hollow center. Start from the right side of the left "teardrop" and weave the long side of the modified *pan chang* knot in an anticlockwise direction. Leave the rest of the cord or use it to tie the inner side of the knot. Take another cord and, starting with the left side of the right "teardrop," weave the other long side of the modified *pan chang* knot in a clockwise direction. Use the rest of the cord to tie the outer side of the knot.

2. Take another cord and tie the inner circle of the knot. This saves time and avoids getting the cord sections mixed up.

3. Make the necklace loop with two new cords. Tie a double connection knot to join the cords. Then, using one cord as the axis, twist the other cord around it to make the loop thicker. At a suitable point along the cord, tie a series of double connection knots. Alternate the cords as axis and repeat the process. Finally, tie a button knot.

52

TYING INSTRUCTIONS

1. Tie two overlapping *hui ling* knots to form a hexagonal love knot. See the instructions on page 94, *Fun with Chinese Knotting.*

2. For the necklace loop, fold a cord and tie a button knot, leaving a loop for hook-up. Use one cord as the axis and twist the other around it to thicken the necklace loop. At various points along the hoop, tie a double connection knot. Alternate the cords as axis and repeat the process. Hook up the love knot formation with the necklace loop and tie a round brocade knot followed by a button knot in the center.

53

TYING INSTRUCTIONS

1. Using the *hui ling* knotting technique, first tie the top *hui ling* knot. On completion of the outer side, take another cord to tie the inner side and the round brocade knot within it. Tighten the knot once it is completed to save on cord.

2. Use the cord ends on the outer side to complete the last corner of the first *hui ling* knot. Then, pull the cord ends through the inner side of the first *hui ling* knot into the big central *hui ling* knot and separately complete both inner sides of this big knot. Use the cord ends to make the inner sides and the central round brocade knot of the *hui ling* knots on the left and right of the central knot.

3. Pull the cord ends from the left and right *hui ling* knots back into the big central one and complete its inner sides and the big round brocade knot, then complete the last *hui ling* knot.

4. Fold another long cord and tie a button knot. Leave a loop for hook-up. Use one cord as the axis and twist the other one around it to thicken the necklace loop. At a suitable length, tie three consecutive double connection knots. Then alternate the cords as axis and repeat the thickening process. Hook up the *hui ling* knot formation and finally tie a button knot.

5. Set beads in the round brocade knots.

54

TYING INSTRUCTIONS

1. First, tie the bottommost cloverleaf knot and a round brocade knot with sixteen outer loops. Wrap every third loop. Then tie a few cloverleaf knots using both cord ends. Separate the cord ends and tie a round brocade knot on either side using the brocade ball knotting technique (see page 62, *Chinese Knotting*). But before doing this, tie the third cloverleaf knot, then, together with the outer loop of the first round broacde knot, tie a double connection knot and leave a suitable length to tie the round brocade knot in the center. Use the cord length left behind and both cord ends to tie the round brocade knot in the center. Then use both cord ends to tie the final round brocade knot followed by a cloverleaf knot. But before tying the final round brocade knot, separately tie each cord end into the first cloverleaf knot, then, together with the outer loop of the round brocade knot on either side, tie a double connection knot.

2. Use two new cords to tie the necklace loop. Tie a double connection knot to hook up the knot formation. Then, alternating one cord as the axis, twist the other one around it to thicken the loop and also to hide the cord ends. Finally, tie a button knot.

3. Tie two round brocade knots with extended cloverleaf knots for the earrings.

55

TYING INSTRUCTIONS

1. Use both cord ends to tie a *ru yi* knot, a *pan chang* knot (though knotted first, the former can only be completed after the latter is completed), and a button knot. Separate both cord ends to separately tie a creeper knot followed by a button knot. Hide the cord ends inside the knot bodies. Twist the outer loop into the desired shape. (Sometimes, if the cord section left behind is too long, the outer loop formed tends to be big and clumsy. Since this is quite difficult to tighten, it can always be twisted it into an elegant design.)

2. Use both cord ends to tie a cloverleaf knot followed by a round brocade knot. (Though knotted first, the former can only be completed after the latter has been done.)

3. Use a thick cord to make the necklace loop.

4. Tie two *pan chang* knots for the earrings.

56

TYING INSTRUCTIONS

1. Tie both cord ends into a cloverleaf knot followed by the body of a *pan chang* knot with a 180-degree shift (though knotted first, the former cannot be completed until the latter is done). Then tie the *pan chang* knot. Hook up this knot formation with a necklace loop.

2. Fold another cord and tie a cloverleaf knot using both cord ends. Make each cord on either side into two ear loops. On each loop, tie a cloverleaf knot and a good luck knot using the technique of pressing small ear loops. Make a suitable design according to the size of the outer loop. Do not tighten to avoid cord abrasion.

57

TYING INSTRUCTIONS

1. Tie both cord ends into a cloverleaf knot, a round brocade knot, a *pan chang* good luck knot and a button knot (turn back the cord ends to make another round). Tie a single cord end into a double connection knot and hide the cord end inside the button knot.

2. Make a thicker cord into the necklace loop.

3. Tie two *lingzhi* knots linked to *pan chang* knots for the earrings.

58 This knot formation should be hung freely to emphasize its body, which is made from a 3D *pan chang* knot. Some of the outer loops can be embellished with red threads to stiffen them and make the knot formation more striking.

TYING INSTRUCTIONS

1. Tie a button knot followed by a *pan chang* knot. Pull out the cord sections in the body of the *pan chang* knot and embellish them with red threads.
2. To make the main knot formation, tie a 3D button knot on the top and bottom part. Then tie a double connection knot above and below each 3D button knot. Right in the center is the pagoda-shaped modified *pan chang* knot. Use its outer loop and the cord sections of its knot body, together with the outer loops from the cloverleaf knots extended from the top and bottom 3D button knots, to tie some more cloverleaf knots. Tie separately some round brocade knots and other cloverleaf knots on the outer loops of the main knot body as well as on the cord sections of its knot body for decorative effect.
3. Break the cord into individual threads and add some red threads to form a tassel.

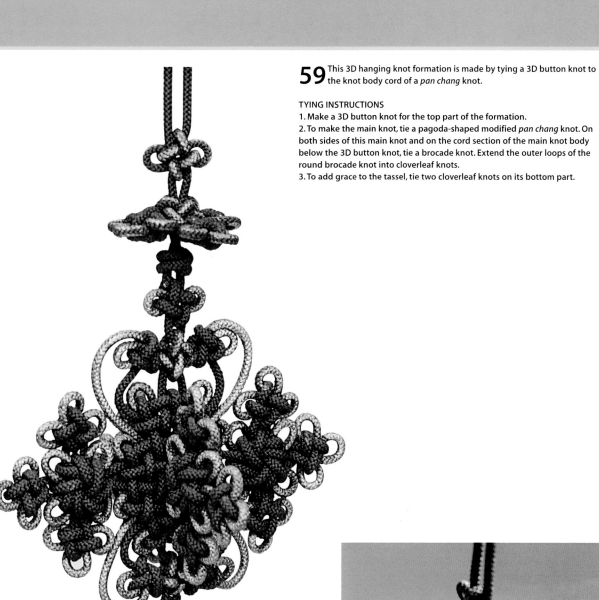

59 This 3D hanging knot formation is made by tying a 3D button knot to the knot body cord of a *pan chang* knot.

TYING INSTRUCTIONS
1. Make a 3D button knot for the top part of the formation.
2. To make the main knot, tie a pagoda-shaped modified *pan chang* knot. On both sides of this main knot and on the cord section of the main knot body below the 3D button knot, tie a brocade knot. Extend the outer loops of the round brocade knot into cloverleaf knots.
3. To add grace to the tassel, tie two cloverleaf knots on its bottom part.

60 The main knot in this hanging formation is a modified *pan chang* knot with a hollow center, i.e. a *hui ling* knot. It has sixteen spaces in which to display different knotting skills. For variation, different color cords for each space or each group of spaces can be used.

TYING INSTRUCTIONS
1. Use both cord ends and work from two different directions to make a *hui ling* knot. See page 90, *Fun with Chinese Knotting*, for instructions.
2. Use different cords to tie the inner sides. On completion of the outer sides of each *hui ling* knot, tie the inner side immediately to avoid a loose formation and messiness. If you prefer not to tie in a separate cord in each space, you should plan in advance to avoid excessive weaving of cord within the knot body.

61 This 3D hanging knot is made by developing side knots on the cord sections on all four sides of a button knot to make the knot formation spread laterally and also to make the button knot body very tight.

TYING INSTRUCTIONS
1. Tie knots in the following order: a 3D button knot, a double connection knot and a *pan chang* knot.
2. Then tie knots in this order: a double connection knot, a *lingzhi* knot on the cord section surrounding each side of the button knot, and a double connection knot.
3. Next tie a *lingzhi* knot on both sides of the *hui ling* knot. Tie a round brocade knot within the *hui ling* knot. Then tie a double connection knot just below the *hui ling* knot.
4. Tie a double connection knot below the 3D button knot.
5. Shellac the entire knot formation to make it shine and to stiffen it. Lastly, paint the silhouetted cords on the knot formation with gold paint.

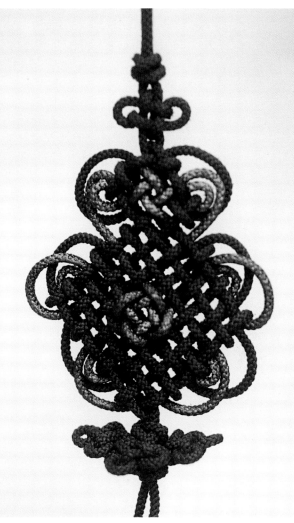

62 This knot formation is an excellent teaching aid because it combines the knotting techniques of the *pan chang* knot with shared ear loops, the shiftweave *pan chang* knot, as well as the *pan chang* knot with compound and overlapping outer loops. The special weaves are highlighted with a different color paint to give the formation an owl-like appearance. The formation is suitable for hanging on a wall.

TYING INSTRUCTIONS
1. Tie a big and a small shiftweave *pan chang* knot, the former with a one up, one down 180-degree shift, and the latter with a two up, two down 90-degree shift. Combine the two using the ear loop sharing technique.
2. Tie a button knot below the main knot as a seat for the "owl." However, there should be no cloverleaf knot on the side of the formation next to the wall.

63 This is a semi-3D knot formation suitable for hanging on a wall. Only the tying method of the main knot is described here.

TYING INSTRUCTIONS
1. First, tie a 3D button knot at the top, but do not tie a cloverleaf knot on the side next to the wall. Then tie a double connection knot above and below the button knot.
2. Tie a *hui ling* knot with eight ear loops on each side. Tie the second and sixth ear loop on each side of the knot, together with each coincided outer loop on the cloverleaf knot extending from each side of the button knot, into cloverleaf knots with two outer loops. Lengthen the fourth ear loop on each side in preparation for tying a cloverleaf knot with two outer loops with the outer loop of the central round brocade knot.
3. When tying the inner side of the *hui ling* knot, upon completing the third ear loop on each side, immediately tie it together with the lengthened fourth loop mentioned in step 2 above into a cloverleaf knot with two outer loops.
4. Lastly, tie the central round brocade knot. Place the pre-tied cloverleaf knot with two outer loops upon the outer loop of the round brocade knot.

64 This knot formation is made by combining the knotting techniques of the *pan chang* knot with compound/overlapped outer loops, the *hui ling* knot and the shiftweave *pan chang* knot.

TYING INSTRUCTIONS
1. Tie a *hui ling* knot with compound and overlapped outer loops.
2. Tie the inner side of the knot with another cord. Use an ear loop from each side and the knotting technique of one up, one down, 180-degree shiftweave *pan chang* knot to tie the central knot.
3. Use the remaining cord ends from the inner and outer sides to tie a round brocade knot as the tassel.

65 This knot formation is made using the *pan chang* knot with compound outer loops, the *pan chang* knot with overlapped outer loops and the shiftweave *pan chang* knot.

TYING INSTRUCTIONS
1. Use three ear loops on each side to tie three groups of 180-degree shiftweave *pan chang* knots. The central group is two up, two down and the top and bottom groups are both one up, one down. The ear loops are arranged according to the knotting technique of the *pan chang* knot with compound/overlapped outer loops.
2. At the bottom, tie a small good luck knot with six outer loops using the pull and wrap technique.
3. Use the remaining cords to tie a tassel with a button knot on each end.

66 This plafond knot formation is designed as a wall hanging wall and hence the side touching the wall is flat. The main knot uses a technique similar to that of the brocade ball knot. In this case, the tightening process changes the shape of the knot formation. Only the main knot is described here.

TYING INSTRUCTIONS
1. When tying the brocade ball knot, tie each outer loop of the first cloverleaf knot with two outer loops into a cloverleaf knot. Use one outer loop from the latter to tie, together with the outer loop of the *pan chang* knot above it, a cloverleaf knot with two outer loops, and lengthen the central loop in preparation for tying a double connection knot together with an adjoining outer loop.
2. Use the two cord ends to tie the knots on the left and right sides. Before tying the second knot unit on the left and the third knot unit on the right, tie a cloverleaf knot on the joining cord. Leave a suitable length of cord for tying the central round brocade knot.
3. For the second knot unit on the left, leave a longer cord length, then use a single cord end and together with the lengthened loop in unit one, tie a double coin knot, a cloverleaf knot (place the double coin knot on the central outer loop of the cloverleaf knot), a round brocade knot (with three outer loops extended into cloverleaf knots), a cloverleaf knot (leave a longer central loop to tie a double coin knot together with adjoining outer loop), and lastly the central cloverleaf knot (with the knot preceding it put upon its third outer loop). Use this same method to tie the third knot unit on the right.
4. Tie each cord end into a cloverleaf knot, then the central round brocade knot.
5. Tie the left (right) cord end, together with the lengthened outer loops in knot units two and three, to tie a double coin knot followed by a cloverleaf knot (place the former upon the latter's central outer loop). Finally, unite both cord ends to tie the central cloverleaf knot and complete the fourth unit in the bottom part.

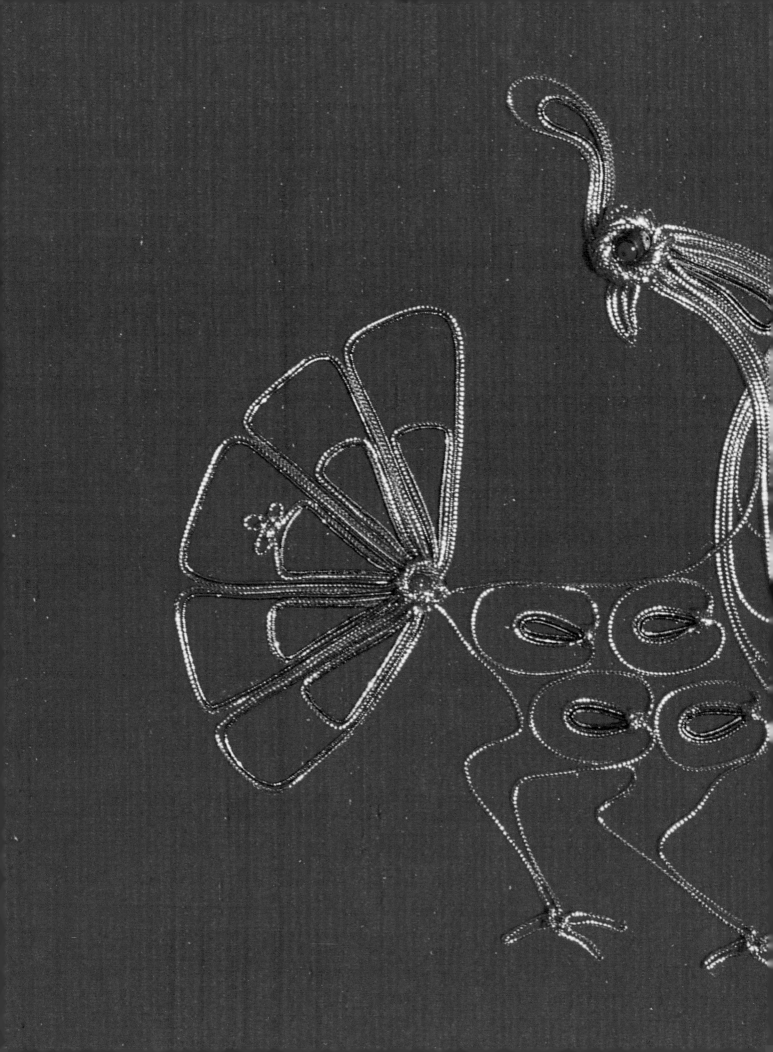